Pictured on the front cover: Chocolate Cake *(page 64)*.

Pictured on the back cover: Cherry Pink Cupcakes *(page 72)*.

Photographs on front cover and pages 62, 113 and 132 copyright ©Shutterstock.com.

ISBN: 978-1-68022-526-6

Library of Congress Control Number: 2016936455

Manufactured in China.

8 7 6 5 4 3 2 1

Microwave Cooking: Microwave ovens vary in wattage. Use the cooking times as guidelines and check for doneness before adding more time.

Publications International, Ltd.

GREAT
BAKING

TABLE OF CONTENTS

SWEET TREATS

COOKIES

Classic Chocolate Chip Cookies — 9
Ginger Molasses Thins — 10
Shortbread Cookies — 11
Pumpkin White Chocolate Drops — 12
Snickerdoodles — 14
Basic Oatmeal Cookies — 15

Classic Thumbprints — 16
Mocha Brownie Cookies — 17
Chocolate-Coconut-Toffee Cookies — 18
Deep Dark Chocolate Drops — 20
Refrigerator Cookies — 21

Black and White Sandwich Cookies — 22
Gingerbread Letters — 24
Meringue Powder Royal Icing — 24
Cocoa Crackles — 26
Chocolate Raspberry Thumbprints — 27

BROWNIES AND BARS

Lemon Squares — 29
Chocolate Chip Skillet Cookie — 30
Mocha Cinnamon Blondies — 31
Mississippi Mud Bars — 32
Easy Layered Bars — 33

Toffee Bars — 34
Caramel Bacon Nut Brownies — 35
Tangy Lemon Raspberry Bars — 36
Cinnamon-Wheat Brownies — 37
Chocolate Dream Bars — 38

Apricot Bars — 39
Chocolate Caramel Bars — 40
Sour Cream Brownies — 41

PIES AND TARTS

Apple-Pear Praline Pie — 43
Pastry for Double-Crust Pie — 43
Peach Raspberry Pie — 44
Pastry for Single-Crust Pie — 44
Banana-Coconut Cream Pie — 46
Turtle Pecan Pie — 47

Lemon Tart — 48
Strawberry-Rhubarb Pie — 49
Fresh Fruit Tart — 50
Maple Pecan Tart — 52
Lattice-Topped Cherry Pie — 53
Lemon Meringue Pie — 54

Country Pecan Pie — 56
Swedish Apple Pie — 57
Italian Chocolate Pie alla Lucia — 58
Sweetened Whipped Cream — 58
Chocolate Curls — 58
Praline Pumpkin Tart — 60

CAKES AND CUPCAKES

Caramel-Topped Cream Cake — 63
Caramel Topping — 63
Buttery Frosting — 63
Chocolate Cake — 64
Ganache Frosting — 64
Marbled Pumpkin Cheesecake — 66
Gingersnap Cookie Crust — 66

Ginger Stout Cake — 68
Blueberry Crumb Cake — 69
Chocolate Espresso Cake — 70
Espresso Chocolate Frosting — 70
Chocolate Buttercream Frosting — 70
Cherry Pink Cupcakes — 72
Cherry Pink Frosting — 72

Orange-Almond Pound Cake — 74
Banana Cake — 75
Classic Yellow Cake — 76
Creamy White Frosting — 76
Chocolate Hazelnut Delight — 78
Porter Cake — 80
Cranberry Pound Cake — 81

DESSERTS

Warm Apple and Blueberry Crisp — 83
Chocolate-Raspberry Bread Pudding — 84
Strawberry-Rhubarb Crisp — 85
Mini Strawberry Shortcakes — 86

Chocolate Crème Brûlée — 88
Cherry-Almond Clafouti — 89
Chocolate Peanut Butter Doughnuts — 90
Blueberry Shortcake — 92

Plum-Rhubarb Crumble — 94
English Bread Pudding — 95
Crunch Peach Cobbler — 96

BREADS AND BEYOND

YEAST BREADS

Spanikopita Pull-Aparts — 101
Pretzel Rolls — 102
Egg Bagels — 104
Cinnamon Rolls — 106

Cardamom Rolls — 108
Banana-Pecan Swirl — 110
Bagels — 112
No-Knead Sandwich Bread — 114

Pesto Pull-Apart Swirls — 115
Anadama Bread — 116
Cinnamon Raisin Bread — 118
Crunchy Whole Grain Bread — 120

QUICK BREADS

Cranberry Pumpkin Nut Bread — 123
Loaded Banana Bread — 124
Blueberry-Apricot Streusel Bread — 126
Lemon Curd — 126
Date Nut Bread — 128

Zucchini Bread — 129
Corn Bread — 130
Honey Butter — 130
Boston Black Coffee Bread — 131
Irish Soda Bread — 132

Citrus Bread — 133
Rhubarb Bread — 134
Blueberry Pecan Tea Bread — 136
Wheat Germ Bread — 137

MUFFINS, SCONES AND DOUGHNUTS

Blueberry Doughnuts — 139
Pumpkin Pecan Muffins — 140
Caramelized Onion-Bacon Muffins — 141
Lemon Poppy Seed Muffins — 142
Sugar and Spice Doughnuts — 144

English-Style Scones — 146
Raspberry Corn Muffins — 147
Sour Cream Doughnuts — 148
Streusel Raspberry Muffins — 150
Orange-Currant Scones — 151
Lemon-Filled Doughnuts — 152

Peanut Butter Bran Muffins — 154
Cherry-Lemon Poppy Seed Muffins — 155
Coconut Scones with Orange Butter — 156
Orange Butter — 156

COFFEECAKES AND BRUNCH BREADS

Cinnamini Monkey Bread — 159
Cherry, Almond and Chocolate Twist — 160
Triple Chocolate Sticky Buns — 162

Orange Poppy Seed Sweet Rolls — 164
Apple Ring Coffeecake — 165
Cherry Buttermilk Loops — 166

Pecan-Cinnamon Sticky Buns — 168
Maple Bacon Bubble Bread — 170
Raspberry Breakfast Ring — 172

SWEET AND SAVORY SNACKS

Pull-Apart Garlic Cheese Bread — 175
Honey Butter Pull-Apart Bread — 176
Mini Pain au Chocolate — 177
Pretzel Bites with Honey Mustard — 178

Belgian Leige Waffles — 180
Graham Crackers — 182
Parmesan and Pine Nut Shortbread — 183

Cranberry Brie Bubble Bread — 184
Cheddar Crisps — 185
Soft Beer Pretzels — 186
Korean Scallion Pancake Waffles — 187

ETC.

Index — 188

Metric conversion chart — 192

SWEET TREATS

COOKIES 8

BROWNIES AND BARS................................. 28

PIES AND TARTS 42

CAKES AND CUPCAKES 62

DESSERTS 82

COOKIES

CLASSIC CHOCOLATE CHIP COOKIES

MAKES ABOUT 2 DOZEN COOKIES

1¼ cups all-purpose flour

½ teaspoon salt

½ teaspoon baking soda

½ cup (1 stick) butter, softened

½ cup granulated sugar

¼ cup packed brown sugar

1 egg

1 teaspoon vanilla

1 cup semisweet chocolate chips

Coarse salt

1. Preheat oven to 350°F. Line cookie sheets with parchment paper.

2. Combine flour, ½ teaspoon salt and baking soda in medium bowl.

3. Attach flat beater to stand mixer. Beat butter, granulated sugar and brown sugar in mixer bowl on medium speed until light and fluffy. Add egg and vanilla; beat until well blended. Add flour mixture; beat just until blended. Stir in chocolate chips. Drop tablespoonfuls of dough 2 inches apart onto prepared cookie sheets. Sprinkle tops with coarse salt.

4. Bake 10 to 12 minutes or until edges are lightly browned. Cool on cookie sheets 1 minute. Remove to wire racks; cool completely.

Note: For best flavor, wrap dough in plastic wrap and refrigerate overnight or up to 3 days.

GINGER MOLASSES THINS

MAKES ABOUT 2½ DOZEN COOKIES

1¼ cups all-purpose flour

1½ teaspoons ground ginger

½ teaspoon salt

½ teaspoon baking soda

½ teaspoon ground cinnamon

⅛ teaspoon ground cloves

½ cup (1 stick) butter, softened

½ cup packed brown sugar

¼ cup granulated sugar

1 egg

2 tablespoons molasses

1 teaspoon vanilla

Coarse white decorating sugar

1. Preheat oven to 350°F. Lightly grease cookie sheets. Combine flour, ginger, salt, baking soda, cinnamon and cloves in medium bowl.

2. Attach flat beater to stand mixer. Beat butter, brown sugar and granulated sugar in mixer bowl on medium speed until light and fluffy. Add egg, molasses and vanilla; beat until well blended. Add flour mixture; beat until well blended.

3. Shape dough by level tablespoons into balls. Roll in decorating sugar; place 2 inches apart on prepared cookie sheets.

4. Bake about 10 minutes or until edges are lightly browned. Cool on cookie sheets 1 minute. Remove to wire racks; cool completely.

SHORTBREAD COOKIES

MAKES 2½ DOZEN COOKIES

- **1 cup (2 sticks) butter, softened**
- **½ cup powdered sugar**
- **2 tablespoons packed brown sugar**
- **½ teaspoon vanilla**
- **¼ teaspoon salt**
- **2 cups all-purpose flour**

1. Attach flat beater to stand mixer. Beat butter, powdered sugar, brown sugar and salt in mixer bowl on medium speed 2 minutes or until light and fluffy. Add vanilla, if desired. Add flour, ½ cup at a time, beating well after each addition. Shape dough into 14-inch-long log. Wrap tightly in plastic wrap; refrigerate 1 hour.

2. Preheat oven to 300°F. Cut dough into ½-inch-thick slices; place on ungreased cookie sheets.

3. Bake 20 to 25 minutes or until lightly browned. Cool on cookie sheets 5 minutes. Remove to wire racks; cool completely.

Note: This dough can be stored in the refrigerator for up to 2 days or in the freezer for a month. If frozen, thaw the dough log in the refrigerator overnight before slicing and baking.

PUMPKIN WHITE CHOCOLATE DROPS

MAKES ABOUT 3 DOZEN COOKIES

1 **cup granulated sugar**

1 **cup (2 sticks) butter, softened**

½ **(15-ounce) can pumpkin puree**

1 **egg**

2 **cups all-purpose flour**

1 **teaspoon pumpkin pie spice***

½ **teaspoon baking powder**

¼ **teaspoon baking soda**

1 **cup white chocolate chips**

FROSTING

½ **cup (1 stick) butter, softened**

4 **ounces cream cheese, softened**

2¼ **cups powdered sugar**

Or substitute ½ teaspoon ground cinnamon, ¼ teaspoon ground ginger, ⅛ teaspoon ground allspice and ⅛ teaspoon ground nutmeg.

1. Preheat oven to 375°F. Line cookie sheets with parchment paper.

2. Attach flat beater to stand mixer. Beat granulated sugar and 1 cup butter in mixer bowl on medium speed until light and fluffy. Add pumpkin and egg; beat until well blended. Add flour, pumpkin pie spice, baking powder and baking soda; beat just until blended. Stir in white chocolate chips. Drop dough by tablespoonfuls about 2 inches apart onto prepared cookie sheets.

3. Bake 16 minutes or until set and lightly browned. Cool on cookie sheets 1 minute. Remove to wire racks; cool completely.

4. For frosting, beat ½ cup butter and cream cheese in bowl of stand mixer on medium speed about 3 minutes or until well blended. Add powdered sugar; beat until creamy.

5. Spread frosting over cookies.

SNICKERDOODLES

MAKES ABOUT 2 DOZEN COOKIES

- 1 **cup sugar, divided**
- 2 **teaspoons ground cinnamon, divided**
- 1⅓ **cups all-purpose flour**
- 1 **teaspoon cream of tartar**
- ½ **teaspoon baking soda**
- ½ **teaspoon salt**
- ½ **cup (1 stick) butter, softened**
- 1 **egg**

1. Preheat oven to 375°F. Line cookie sheets with parchment paper. Combine ¼ cup sugar and 1 teaspoon cinnamon in small bowl.

2. Combine flour, remaining 1 teaspoon cinnamon, cream of tartar, baking soda and salt in medium bowl.

3. Attach flat beater to stand mixer. Beat remaining ¾ cup sugar and butter in mixer bowl on medium speed until creamy. Beat in egg. Gradually add flour mixture, beating on low speed until stiff dough forms. Roll dough into 1-inch balls; roll in cinnamon-sugar mixture. Place 2 inches apart on prepared cookie sheets.

4. Bake 10 minutes or just until set. Remove to wire racks; cool completely.

BASIC OATMEAL COOKIES

MAKES 3 DOZEN COOKIES

- 2 **cups old-fashioned oats**
- 1⅓ **cups all-purpose flour**
- ¾ **teaspoon baking soda**
- ½ **teaspoon baking powder**
- 1 **teaspoon salt**
- 1 **cup packed brown sugar**
- ¾ **cup (1½ sticks) butter, softened**
- ¼ **cup granulated sugar**
- 1 **egg**
- 1 **tablespoon honey**
- 1 **teaspoon vanilla**

1. Preheat oven to 350°F. Line cookie sheets with parchment paper.

2. Combine oats, flour, baking soda, baking powder and salt in medium bowl.

3. Attach flat beater to stand mixer. Beat brown sugar, butter and granulated sugar in mixer bowl on medium speed until light and fluffy. Add egg, honey and vanilla; beat until well blended. Gradually add flour mixture, beating at low speed just until blended. Drop dough by tablespoonfuls about 2 inches apart onto prepared cookie sheets.

4. Bake 11 to 15 minutes or just until cookies are puffed and golden. Cool on cookie sheets 5 minutes. Remove to wire racks; cool completely.

CLASSIC THUMBPRINTS

MAKES ABOUT 3 DOZEN COOKIES

1 cup (2 sticks) butter, softened

½ cup powdered sugar

2 tablespoons packed brown sugar

¼ teaspoon salt

1 egg

½ teaspoon vanilla

2 cups all-purpose flour

¼ cup strawberry, grape or apricot jam

1. Attach flat beater to stand mixer. Beat butter, powdered sugar, brown sugar and salt in mixer bowl on medium speed 2 minutes or until light and fluffy. Add egg and vanilla; beat until well blended.

2. Add flour, ½ cup at a time, beating well after each addition. Shape dough into disc; wrap in plastic wrap. Refrigerate 1 hour or until firm.

3. Preheat oven to 300°F.

4. Shape dough into 1-inch balls; place 1 inch apart on ungreased cookie sheets. Make small indentation in each ball with thumb; fill with heaping ¼ teaspoon jam.

5. Bake 12 to 15 minutes or until light golden brown. Cool on cookie sheets 1 minute. Remove to wire racks; cool completely.

MOCHA BROWNIE COOKIES

MAKES 5 TO 6 DOZEN COOKIES

2½ cups all-purpose flour
⅓ cup unsweetened cocoa powder
1 teaspoon baking soda
1 teaspoon baking powder
1 teaspoon salt
1 cup granulated sugar
¾ cup packed brown sugar
½ cup (1 stick) butter, softened
¼ cup sour cream
1 tablespoon instant coffee granules, dissolved in 2 tablespoons hot water
2 eggs
1½ cups semisweet chocolate chips

1. Preheat oven to 325°F. Combine flour, cocoa, baking soda, baking powder and salt in medium bowl.

2. Attach flat beater to stand mixer. Beat granulated sugar, brown sugar, butter, sour cream and coffee mixture in mixer bowl on medium speed until creamy. Add eggs, one at a time, beating well after each addition. Gradually add flour mixture, beating on low speed just until blended. Beat on medium speed 1 minute. Stir in chocolate chips. Drop dough by rounded tablespoonfuls onto ungreased cookie sheets.

3. Bake 9 to 11 minutes or until slight imprint remains when pressed with finger. Cool on cookie sheets 3 minutes. Remove to wire racks; cool completely.

CHOCOLATE–COCONUT–TOFFEE COOKIES

MAKES 1 DOZEN LARGE COOKIES

½ cup all-purpose flour

¼ teaspoon baking powder

¼ teaspoon salt

1 package (12 ounces) semisweet chocolate chips, divided

¼ cup (½ stick) butter, cut into small pieces

¾ cup packed brown sugar

2 eggs

1 teaspoon vanilla

1½ cups flaked coconut

1 cup toffee baking bits

½ cup bittersweet chocolate chips

1. Preheat oven to 350°F. Line cookie sheets with parchment paper. Combine flour, baking powder and salt in small bowl.

2. Place 1 cup semisweet chocolate chips and butter in large microwavable bowl. Microwave on HIGH 1 minute; stir. Microwave at additional 30-second intervals, stirring after each interval, until mixture is melted and smooth.

3. Attach flat beater to stand mixer. Beat brown sugar, eggs and vanilla in mixer bowl on medium speed until well blended. Beat in chocolate mixture until well blended. Add flour mixture; beat on low speed until blended. Stir in coconut, toffee bits and remaining 1 cup semisweet chocolate chips. Drop dough by heaping ⅓ cupfuls 3 inches apart onto prepared cookie sheets. Flatten with rubber spatula into 3½-inch circles.

4. Bake 15 to 17 minutes or until edges are firm. Cool on cookie sheets 2 minutes; slide parchment paper and cookies onto wire racks. Cool completely.

5. For chocolate drizzle, place bittersweet chocolate chips in small microwavable bowl. Microwave on HIGH 30 seconds; stir. Microwave at additional 30-second intervals, stirring after each interval, until melted and smooth. Drizzle over cookies using fork. Let stand until set.

DEEP DARK CHOCOLATE DROPS

MAKES ABOUT 3 DOZEN COOKIES

1¼ cups all-purpose flour

¼ cup unsweetened cocoa powder

½ teaspoon baking soda

½ teaspoon salt

1½ cups semisweet chocolate chips, divided

½ cup (1 stick) butter, softened

½ cup granulated sugar

¼ cup packed brown sugar

1 egg

2 tablespoons milk

1 teaspoon vanilla

1. Preheat oven to 350°F. Line cookie sheets with parchment paper. Combine flour, cocoa, baking soda and salt in medium bowl.

2. Place ½ cup chocolate chips in small microwavable bowl. Microwave on HIGH 1 minute; stir. Microwave at additional 30-second intervals, stirring after each interval, until melted and smooth. Cool slightly.

3. Attach flat beater to stand mixer. Beat butter, granulated sugar and brown sugar in mixer bowl on medium speed until light and fluffy. Add egg, milk, vanilla and melted chocolate; beat until well blended. Add flour mixture; beat on low speed just until blended. Stir in remaining 1 cup chocolate chips.

4. Drop dough by rounded tablespoonfuls 2 inches apart onto prepared cookie sheets.

5. Bake 10 minutes or until set. Cool on cookie sheets 2 minutes. Remove to wire racks; cool completely.

REFRIGERATOR COOKIES

MAKES ABOUT 4 DOZEN COOKIES

1¾ **cups all-purpose flour**

¼ **teaspoon baking soda**

¼ **teaspoon salt**

½ **cup sugar**

¼ **cup light corn syrup**

¼ **cup (½ stick) butter, softened**

1 **egg**

1 **teaspoon vanilla**

Decorating sugars and decors

1. Combine flour, baking soda and salt in medium bowl.

2. Attach flat beater to stand mixer. Beat sugar, corn syrup and butter in mixer bowl on medium speed until well blended. Add egg and vanilla; mix well. Add flour mixture; mix on low speed until well blended. Shape dough into two logs 1½ inches in diameter. Wrap in plastic wrap. Freeze 1 hour.

3. Preheat oven to 350°F. Line baking sheets with parchment paper. Cut dough into ¼-inch-thick slices; place 1 inch apart on prepared cookie sheets. Sprinkle with decors, if desired.

4. Bake 8 to 10 minutes or until edges are golden brown. Remove to wire racks; cool completely.

BLACK AND WHITE SANDWICH COOKIES

MAKES ABOUT 3½ DOZEN COOKIES

COOKIES

- 1¼ cups (2½ sticks) butter
- ¾ cup superfine or granulated sugar
- 1 egg
- 1½ teaspoons vanilla
- ¼ teaspoon salt
- 2⅓ cups all-purpose flour, divided
- ⅓ cup unsweetened cocoa powder

FILLING

- ½ cup (1 stick) butter, softened
- 4 ounces cream cheese, softened
- 2 cups plus 2 tablespoons powdered sugar
- 2 tablespoons unsweetened cocoa powder

1. For cookies, attach flat beater to stand mixer. Beat 1¼ cups butter and superfine sugar in mixer bowl on medium speed until creamy. Beat in egg, vanilla and salt until well blended. Add 2 cups flour; mix on low speed until combined.

2. Remove half of dough to medium bowl; stir in remaining ⅓ cup flour. Add ⅓ cup cocoa to dough in mixer bowl; beat just until blended. Wrap doughs separately in plastic wrap; refrigerate 30 minutes or until firm.

3. Preheat oven to 350°F. Line two cookie sheets with parchment paper. Roll out plain dough on floured surface to ¼-inch thickness. Cut out 1-inch circles; place 2 inches apart on prepared cookie sheet. Repeat with chocolate dough.

4. Bake 8 to 10 minutes. Remove to wire racks; cool completely.

5. For filling, beat ½ cup butter and cream cheese in bowl of stand mixer on medium speed about 3 minutes or until well blended. Add 2 cups powdered sugar; beat until creamy. Remove half of filling to small bowl; stir in remaining 2 tablespoons powdered sugar. Add 2 tablespoons cocoa to filling in mixer bowl; beat until smooth.

6. Pipe or spread chocolate frosting on flat side of half of plain cookies; top with remaining plain cookies. Pipe or spread plain frosting on flat side of half of chocolate cookies; top with remaining chocolate cookies.

GINGERBREAD LETTERS

MAKES ABOUT 5 DOZEN COOKIES

1½ cups all-purpose flour

1 teaspoon ground cinnamon

½ teaspoon baking soda

½ teaspoon salt

½ teaspoon ground ginger

¼ teaspoon baking powder

½ cup (1 stick) butter, softened

⅓ cup packed brown sugar

¼ cup molasses

1 egg white

½ teaspoon vanilla

Meringue Powder Royal Icing (recipe follows)

Assorted decors (optional)

1. Combine flour, cinnamon, baking soda, salt, ginger and baking powder in small bowl.

2. Attach flat beater to stand mixer. Beat butter, brown sugar, molasses, egg white and vanilla in mixer bowl on high speed until smooth. Add flour mixture; mix on low speed until well blended. Wrap with plastic wrap; refrigerate at least 1 hour or until firm.

3. Preheat oven to 350°F. Line cookie sheets with parchment paper.

4. Working with one quarter at a time, roll out dough to ⅛-inch thickness on floured surface. Cut out letter shapes using 2½-inch cookie cutters. Place cutouts on prepared cookie sheets.

5. Bake 6 to 8 minutes or until set but not browned. Remove cookies to wire racks; cool completely.

6. Prepare icing; tint desired colors. Fit pastry bags with small tips; fill with icing. Outline cookies and fill in. Decorate with decors.

MERINGUE POWDER ROYAL ICING

¼ cup plus 2 tablespoons water

¼ cup meringue powder*

1 package (16 ounces) powdered sugar, sifted

Meringue powder is available where cake decorating supplies are sold.

1. Attach flat beater to stand mixer. Beat water and meringue powder in mixer bowl on low speed until well blended. Beat on high speed until stiff peaks form.

2. Beat in powdered sugar on low speed until well blended. Beat on medium speed until icing is very stiff. Cover icing with damp cloth to prevent it from drying.

COCOA CRACKLES

MAKES ABOUT 3½ DOZEN COOKIES

- 1½ **cups all-purpose flour**
- ⅓ **cup unsweetened cocoa powder**
- ½ **teaspoon salt**
- ½ **teaspoon baking soda**
- ½ **cup (1 stick) butter, softened**
- ½ **cup granulated sugar**
- ¼ **cup packed brown sugar**
- 2 **eggs**
- 1 **teaspoon vanilla**
  Powdered sugar

1. Preheat oven to 350°F. Line cookie sheets with parchment paper.

2. Combine flour, cocoa, salt and baking soda in medium bowl. Attach flat beater to stand mixer. Beat butter, granulated sugar and brown sugar in mixer bowl on medium speed until light and fluffy. Add eggs and vanilla; beat until well blended. Add flour mixture; beat just until blended.

3. Place powdered sugar in shallow bowl. Shape dough by heaping teaspoons into balls. Roll balls in powdered sugar; place 2 inches apart on prepared cookie sheets.

4. Bake 11 minutes or until set and no longer shiny. Cool on cookie sheets 2 minutes. Remove to wire racks; cool completely.

CHOCOLATE RASPBERRY THUMBPRINTS

MAKES ABOUT 4½ DOZEN COOKIES

1½ cups (3 sticks) butter, softened

1 cup granulated sugar

1 egg

1 teaspoon vanilla

3 cups all-purpose flour

¼ cup unsweetened cocoa powder

½ teaspoon salt

1 cup mini semisweet chocolate chips (optional)

⅔ cup raspberry preserves

Powdered sugar (optional)

1. Preheat oven to 350°F. Line cookie sheets with parchment paper.

2. Attach flat beater to stand mixer. Beat butter and granulated sugar in large bowl. Add egg and vanilla; beat until light and fluffy. Mix in flour, cocoa and salt until well blended. Stir in mini chocolate chips, if desired.

3. Shape level tablespoonfuls of dough into balls. Place 2 inches apart on prepared cookie sheets. Make deep indentation in center of each ball with thumb.

4. Bake 12 to 15 minutes until just set. Cool on cookie sheets 2 minutes. Remove to wire racks; cool completely.

5. Sprinkle with powdered sugar, if desired. Fill centers with raspberry preserves.

BROWNIES AND BARS

LEMON SQUARES

MAKES 2 TO 3 DOZEN BARS

CRUST

- 1 cup (2 sticks) butter, softened
- ½ cup granulated sugar
- ½ teaspoon salt
- 2 cups all-purpose flour

FILLING

- 3 cups granulated sugar
- 1 cup all-purpose flour
- 4 eggs plus 2 egg yolks, at room temperature
- ⅔ cup fresh lemon juice
- 2 tablespoons grated lemon peel
- ½ teaspoon baking powder
  Powdered sugar

1. Attach flat beater to stand mixer. Beat butter, ½ cup granulated sugar and salt in mixer bowl on medium speed until light and fluffy. Add 2 cups flour; mix on low speed just until blended.

2. Press dough into 13×9-inch baking pan, building edges up ½ inch on all sides. Refrigerate 20 minutes or until slightly firm.

3. Preheat oven to 350°F. Bake 15 to 20 minutes or until very lightly browned. Cool on wire rack.

4. Attach wire whip to stand mixer. Whip 3 cups granulated sugar, flour, eggs and egg yolks, sugar, lemon juice, lemon peel, 1 cup flour and baking powder. Pour over crust.

5. Bake 30 to 35 minutes until filling is set. Cool completely in pan on wire rack. Cut into squares; sprinkle with powdered sugar.

CHOCOLATE CHIP SKILLET COOKIE

MAKES 8 SERVINGS

1¾ cups all-purpose flour

1 teaspoon baking soda

1 teaspoon salt

¾ cup (1½ sticks) butter, softened

¾ cup packed brown sugar

½ cup granulated sugar

2 eggs

1 teaspoon vanilla

1 package (12 ounces) semisweet chocolate chips

Coarse sea salt (optional)

Ice cream (optional)

1. Preheat oven to 350°F.

2. Combine flour, baking soda and salt in medium bowl.

3. Attach flat beater to stand mixer. Beat butter, brown sugar and granulated sugar in mixer bowl on medium speed until creamy. Beat in eggs and vanilla until well blended. Gradually beat in flour on low speed just until blended. Stir in chocolate chips.

4. Press batter evenly into well-seasoned large (10-inch) cast iron skillet. Sprinkle lightly with sea salt, if desired.

5. Bake about 35 minutes or until top and edges are golden brown but cookie is still soft in center. Cool on wire rack 10 minutes before cutting into wedges. Serve warm with ice cream, if desired.

MOCHA CINNAMON BLONDIES

MAKES 2 TO 3 DOZEN BLONDIES

1 cup (2 sticks) butter, melted and cooled

1¾ cups sugar

4 eggs

1 cup all-purpose flour

2 teaspoons instant coffee granules

1 teaspoon ground cinnamon

¼ teaspoon salt

1 cup chopped pecans

¾ cup semisweet chocolate chips

1. Preheat oven to 350°F. Grease 13×9-inch baking pan.

2. Attach flat beater to stand mixer. Beat butter, sugar and eggs in mixer bowl on medium speed until light and fluffy. Add flour, coffee, cinnamon and salt; mix on low speed until blended. Stir in pecans and chocolate chips. Spread batter in prepared pan.

3. Bake 30 minutes or until edges begin to pull away from sides of pan. Cool completely in pan on wire rack.

MISSISSIPPI MUD BARS

MAKES 2 TO 3 DOZEN BARS OR TRIANGLES

¾ **cup packed brown sugar**

½ **cup (1 stick) butter, softened**

1 **egg**

1 **teaspoon vanilla**

½ **teaspoon baking soda**

¼ **teaspoon salt**

1 **cup plus 2 tablespoons all-purpose flour**

1 **cup semisweet chocolate chips, divided**

1 **cup white chocolate chips, divided**

½ **cup chopped walnuts or pecans**

1. Preheat oven to 375°F. Line 9-inch square baking pan with foil; grease foil.

2. Attach flat beater to stand mixer. Beat brown sugar and butter in mixer bowl on medium speed until well blended. Beat in egg, vanilla, baking soda and salt until blended. Add flour; mix on low speed until well blended. Stir in ⅔ cup semisweet chips, ⅔ cup white chips and walnuts. Press dough into prepared pan.

3. Bake 23 to 25 minutes or until center is firm to the touch. *Do not overbake.* Sprinkle with remaining ⅓ cup semisweet chips and ⅓ cup white chips. Let stand until chips soften; spread and swirl evenly over bars. Cool in pan on wire rack until chocolate is set. Cut into bars or triangles.

EA

MAKI

1

½

½

1 c

1 cu

¾ cu

¾ cu

1 cup coarsely chopped pecans

1. Preheat oven to 350°F.

2. Attach flat beater to stand mixer. Beat cracker crumbs, oats and butter in mixer bowl until crumbly. Press into 13×9-inch pan. Spread condensed milk over base. Layer coconut, chocolate chips, raisins and pecans over milk.

3. Bake 25 to 30 minutes or until lightly browned. Cool in pan on wire rack 5 minutes; cut into bars. Cool completely in pan on wire rack. Cut into bars.

TOFFEE BARS

MAKES 2 TO 3 DOZEN BARS

- ½ cup (1 stick) butter, softened
- ½ cup packed brown sugar
- 1 egg yolk
- 1 teaspoon vanilla
- 1 cup all-purpose flour
- 1 cup milk chocolate chips
- ½ cup chopped walnuts or pecans

1. Preheat oven to 350°F. Grease 13×9-inch baking pan.

2. Attach flat beater to stand mixer. Beat butter and brown sugar in mixer bowl on medium speed until creamy. Blend in egg yolk and vanilla. Stir in flour until well blended. Press dough into prepared pan.

3. Bake 15 minutes or until golden. Sprinkle evenly with chocolate chips. Let stand several minutes until chips melt; spread chocolate evenly over bars. Sprinkle with walnuts. Score into bars while still warm. Cool completely in pan on wire rack; cut into bars along score lines.

CARAMEL BACON NUT BROWNIES

MAKES 2 TO 3 DOZEN BROWNIES

- ¾ cup (1½ sticks) butter
- 4 ounces unsweetened chocolate
- 2 cups sugar
- 4 eggs
- 1 cup all-purpose flour
- 1 package (14 ounces) caramels
- ¼ cup heavy cream
- 2 cups pecan halves or coarsely chopped pecans, divided
- 4 slices bacon, crisp-cooked and crumbled
- 1 package (12 ounces) chocolate chunks or chips, divided

1. Preheat oven to 350°F. Grease 13×9-inch baking pan. Attach flat beater to stand mixer.

2. Place butter and chocolate in large microwavable bowl. Microwave on HIGH 1½ to 2 minutes or until melted and smooth. Transfer to bowl of stand mixer. Add sugar; beat on medium speed until well blended. Add eggs, one at a time, beating until well blended after each addition. Stir in flour on low speed. Spread half of batter in prepared pan. Bake 20 minutes.

3. Meanwhile, combine caramels and cream in medium microwavable bowl. Microwave on HIGH 1½ minutes or until caramels begin to melt; stir until smooth. Stir in 1 cup pecans and bacon.

4. Spread caramel mixture over partially baked brownie layer. Sprinkle with half of chocolate chunks. Pour remaining batter over top; sprinkle with remaining 1 cup pecans and chocolate chunks. Bake 25 minutes or until set. Cool completely in pan on wire rack. Cut into squares.

TANGY LEMON RASPBERRY BARS

MAKES 12 TO 16 BARS

¾ cup packed brown sugar

½ cup (1 stick) butter, softened

Grated peel of 1 lemon

1 cup all-purpose flour

1 cup old-fashioned oats

1 teaspoon baking powder

½ teaspoon salt

½ cup raspberry jam

1. Preheat oven to 350°F. Grease 8-inch square baking pan.

2. Attach flat beater to stand mixer. Beat brown sugar, butter and lemon peel in mixer bowl on medium speed until combined. Add flour, oats, baking powder and salt; beat on low speed until combined. Reserve ¼ cup mixture. Press remaining mixture into prepared pan. Spread jam over top; sprinkle with reserved mixture.

3. Bake 25 minutes or until edges are lightly browned. Cool completely in pan on wire rack. Cut into bars.

CINNAMON–WHEAT BROWNIES

MAKES 12 TO 16 BROWNIES

2 ounces unsweetened chocolate, chopped

½ cup (1 stick) butter, softened

1 cup packed dark brown sugar

2 eggs

1 teaspoon ground cinnamon

1 teaspoon vanilla

¼ teaspoon baking powder

¼ teaspoon ground ginger

⅛ teaspoon ground cloves

½ cup whole wheat flour

1 cup coarsely chopped walnuts

1. Preheat oven to 350°F. Grease 8-inch square baking pan. Melt chocolate in top of double boiler over simmering water. Cool slightly.

2. Attach flat beater to stand mixer. Beat butter, brown sugar, eggs and melted chocolate in mixer bowl on medium speed until light and fluffy. Stir in cinnamon, vanilla, baking powder, ginger and cloves. Stir in flour and walnuts on low speed until well blended. Spread batter evenly in prepared pan.

3. Bake 25 minutes or until top is firm and dry. Cool completely in pan on wire rack. Cut into squares.

CHOCOLATE DREAM BARS

MAKES ABOUT 4½ DOZEN BARS

1½ cups packed brown sugar, divided

½ cup (1 stick) butter, softened

1 egg yolk

1 cup plus 2 tablespoons all-purpose flour, divided

2 eggs

1 cup semisweet chocolate chips

½ cup chopped toasted walnuts*

*To toast walnuts, spread in single layer on baking sheet. Bake in preheated 350°F oven 5 to 7 minutes or until golden brown, stirring frequently.

1. Preheat oven to 375°F. Grease 13×9-inch baking pan.

2. Attach flat beater to stand mixer. Beat ½ cup brown sugar, butter and egg yolk in mixer bowl on medium speed until light and fluffy. Stir in 1 cup flour until well blended. Press dough into prepared pan. Bake 12 to 15 minutes or until golden.

3. Meanwhile, beat remaining 1 cup brown sugar, 2 tablespoons flour and whole eggs in mixer bowl on medium-high speed until light and frothy. Spread mixture over partially baked crust.

4. Return to oven; bake about 15 minutes or until topping is set. Immediately sprinkle with chocolate chips. Let stand until chips melt, then spread chocolate evenly over bars. Sprinkle with walnuts. Cool completely in pan on wire rack. Cut into bars.

APRICOT BARS

MAKES 12 TO 16 BARS

½ **cup sugar**

½ **cup (1 stick) butter, softened**

2 **eggs**

1 **cup apricot preserves**

1 **teaspoon vanilla**

1 **cup all-purpose flour**

⅔ **cup old-fashioned oats**

1¼ **teaspoons baking powder**

¾ **teaspoon ground cinnamon**

½ **teaspoon salt**

¼ **teaspoon ground allspice**

⅛ **teaspoon ground mace or nutmeg**

1. Preheat oven to 350°F. Grease 13×9-inch baking pan.

2. Attach flat beater to stand mixer. Beat sugar and butter in mixer bowl on medium speed about 1 minute or until well blended. Add eggs, fruit spread and vanilla; beat until combined after each addition. Add flour, oats, baking powder, cinnamon, salt, allspice and mace; mix on low speed until well blended. Spread dough in prepared baking dish.

3. Bake 18 minutes or until golden brown and top is firm. Cool completely in baking pan on wire rack. Cut into bars.

CHOCOLATE CARAMEL BARS

MAKES 2 TO 3 DOZEN BARS

2 cups all-purpose flour

1½ cups packed brown sugar, divided

1¼ cups (2½ sticks) butter, softened, divided

1 cup chopped pecans

1½ cups semisweet chocolate chips

1. Preheat oven to 350°F.

2. Attach flat beater to stand mixer. Beat flour, 1 cup brown sugar and ½ cup butter in mixer bowl on low speed about 1 minute or until crumbly. Press firmly into 13×9-inch pan; sprinkle with pecans.

3. Combine remaining ½ cup brown sugar and ¾ cup butter in medium heavy saucepan. Cook over medium heat until mixture comes to a boil, stirring constantly. Boil 1 minute until blended and smooth, stirring constantly. Pour caramel evenly over pecans and crust.

4. Bake 18 to 20 minutes or until caramel layer bubbles all over. Immediately sprinkle with chocolate chips. Let stand 2 minutes or until chips melt; spread chocolate evenly over bars. Let stand until set; cut into bars.

SOUR CREAM BROWNIES

MAKES 2 TO 3 DOZEN BROWNIES

½ cup (1 stick) butter, softened
1 cup packed brown sugar
1 egg
1 cup sour cream
1 teaspoon vanilla
½ cup unsweetened cocoa powder
½ teaspoon baking soda
¼ teaspoon salt
2 cups all-purpose flour
1 cup semisweet chocolate chips
Powdered sugar (optional)

1. Preheat oven to 350°F. Grease 13×9-inch baking pan.

2. Attach flat beater to stand mixer. Beat butter and brown sugar on medium speed in mixer bowl until creamy. Add egg, sour cream and vanilla; beat until light. Add cocoa, baking soda and salt; beat until smooth. Add flour; beat on low speed until well blended. Stir in chocolate chips. Spread batter evenly in prepared pan.

3. Bake 25 to 30 minutes or until center springs back when touched. Cool in pan on wire rack. Sprinkle with powdered sugar, if desired.

PIES AND TARTS

APPLE–PEAR PRALINE PIE

MAKES 8 SERVINGS

Pastry for Double-Crust Pie (recipe follows)

- 4 cups sliced peeled Granny Smith apples
- 2 cups sliced peeled pears
- ¾ cup granulated sugar
- ¼ cup plus 1 tablespoon all-purpose flour, divided
- 4 teaspoons ground cinnamon
- ¼ teaspoon salt
- ½ cup (1 stick) plus 2 tablespoons butter, divided
- 1 cup packed brown sugar
- 1 tablespoon half-and-half
- 1 cup chopped pecans

1. Prepare pie pastry.

2. Combine apples, pears, granulated sugar, ¼ cup flour, cinnamon and salt in large bowl; toss to coat. Let stand 15 minutes.

3. Preheat oven to 350°F. Roll out one disc of pastry into 11-inch circle on floured surface. Line deep-dish 9-inch pie plate with pastry; sprinkle with remaining 1 tablespoon flour. Spoon fruit mixture into crust; dot with 2 tablespoons butter. Roll out remaining disc of pastry into 10-inch circle. Place over fruit; seal and flute edge. Cut slits in top crust.

4. Bake 1 hour. Meanwhile, combine remaining ½ cup butter, brown sugar and half-and-half in small saucepan; bring to a boil over medium heat, stirring frequently. Boil 2 minutes, stirring constantly. Remove from heat; stir in pecans. Let stand until slightly thickened. Spread over pie.

5. Cool pie on wire rack 15 minutes. Serve warm or at room temperature.

PASTRY FOR DOUBLE–CRUST PIE

MAKES PASTRY FOR ONE DOUBLE–CRUST 9-INCH PIE

- 2½ cups all-purpose flour
- 1 teaspoon salt
- 1 teaspoon sugar
- 1 cup (2 sticks) cold butter, cubed
- 7 tablespoons ice water
- 1 tablespoon cider vinegar

1. Attach flat beater to stand mixer. Combine flour, salt and sugar in mixer bowl. Add butter; mix on low speed 1 minute or until coarse crumbs form. Combine ice water and vinegar in small bowl.

2. With mixer running on low speed, drizzle in enough water mixture just until dough starts to come together. Turn out dough onto lightly floured surface; press into a ball. Divide in half. Shape each half into a disc; wrap in plastic wrap. Refrigerate 30 minutes.

PEACH RASPBERRY PIE

MAKES 8 SERVINGS

Pastry for Single-Crust Pie (recipe follows)

⅔ cup old-fashioned or quick oats

¼ cup all-purpose flour

¼ cup packed brown sugar

¼ cup slivered almonds

1 teaspoon ground cinnamon, divided

3 tablespoons butter, softened

5 cups sliced peaches (about 2 pounds)

2 tablespoons fresh lemon juice

1 cup fresh raspberries

½ cup granulated sugar

2 tablespoons quick-cooking tapioca

¼ teaspoon ground nutmeg

1. Prepare pie pastry. For topping, combine oats, flour, brown sugar, almonds and ½ teaspoon cinnamon in medium bowl. Stir in butter until mixture resembles coarse crumbs.

2. Roll out pastry into 11-inch circle on floured surface. Line 9-inch pie plate with pastry; trim and flute edge. Refrigerate 15 minutes.

3. Preheat oven to 400°F. Place peaches in large bowl. Sprinkle with lemon juice; toss to coat. Gently stir in raspberries.

4. Combine granulated sugar, tapioca, remaining ½ teaspoon cinnamon and nutmeg in small bowl. Sprinkle over fruit mixture; toss to coat. Spread evenly in crust. Sprinkle with topping.

5. Bake 15 minutes. *Reduce oven temperature to 350°F.* Bake 30 minutes or until filling is bubbly. Cool on wire rack 15 minutes. Serve warm or at room temperature.

PASTRY FOR SINGLE-CRUST PIE

MAKES PASTRY FOR ONE 9-INCH PIE

1¼ cups all-purpose flour

½ teaspoon salt

6 tablespoons cold butter, cubed

3 to 4 tablespoons ice water

1 teaspoon cider vinegar

1. Attach flat beater to stand mixer. Combine flour and salt in mixer bowl. Add butter; mix on low speed 1 minute or until coarse crumbs form. Combine ice water and vinegar in small bowl.

2. With mixer running on low speed, drizzle in enough water mixture just until dough starts to come together. Turn out dough onto lightly floured surface. Shape into a disc. Wrap in plastic wrap. Refrigerate 30 minutes.

BANANA–COCONUT CREAM PIE

MAKES 8 SERVINGS

CRUST

- **1 cup almonds**
- **1 tablespoon sugar**
- **½ cup flaked coconut**
- **¼ cup (½ stick) butter, cut into pieces**
- **Pinch salt**

FILLING

- **3 bananas, divided**
- **1 teaspoon lemon juice**
- **½ cup sugar**
- **¼ cup cornstarch**
- **¼ teaspoon salt**
- **3 cups whole milk**
- **2 egg yolks**
- **1 teaspoon vanilla**
- **2 tablespoons flaked coconut, toasted***
- **Sweetened whipped cream (page 58, optional)**

To toast coconut, spread in single layer in heavy-bottomed skillet. Cook over medium heat 1 to 2 minutes, stirring frequently, until lightly browned. Remove from skillet immediately. Cool before using.

1. Preheat oven to 350°F. Grease 9-inch pie pan.

2. Place almonds and 1 tablespoon sugar in food processor; pulse until almonds are ground. Add ½ cup coconut; pulse to combine. Add butter and pinch of salt; pulse until mixture forms clumps. Press mixture onto bottom and up side of prepared pan. Bake 10 to 12 minutes or until golden. Cool completely.

3. Slice 2 bananas; sprinkle with lemon juice. Layer on bottom of prepared crust.

4. Combine ½ cup sugar, cornstarch and ¼ teaspoon salt in small bowl. Attach wire whip to stand mixer. Whip milk and egg yolks in mixer bowl on medium speed until well blended. Reduce speed to low; gradually add sugar mixture.

5. Transfer to medium saucepan. Cook and stir over medium heat until thickened. Bring to a boil; boil 1 minute. Remove from heat; stir in vanilla. Pour mixture over bananas in crust. Cover and refrigerate at least 2 hours or until ready to serve.

6. Slice remaining banana; arrange on top of pie. Garnish with toasted coconut and whipped cream.

TURTLE PECAN PIE

MAKES 8 SERVINGS

Pastry for Single-Crust Pie (page 44)
1 **cup light corn syrup**
3 **eggs, lightly beaten**
½ **cup sugar**
⅓ **cup butter, melted**
1 **teaspoon vanilla**
½ **teaspoon salt**
1¼ **cups pecans, toasted***
2 **ounces semisweet chocolate, melted**
½ **cup caramel ice cream topping**
Sweetened whipped cream (page 58) and grated chocolate (optional)

To toast nuts, place on baking sheet. Bake in preheated 350°F oven 5 to 7 minutes or until lightly browned, stirring occasionally. Immediately remove from pan; cool before using.

1. Prepare pie pastry. Preheat oven to 350°F. Roll out pastry into 11-inch circle on floured surface. Line 9-inch pie plate with pastry; trim and flute edge. Refrigerate 15 minutes. Place on baking sheet.

2. Attach flat beater to stand mixer. Beat corn syrup, eggs, sugar, butter, vanilla and salt in mixer bowl on medium speed until well blended. Reserve ½ cup egg mixture. Stir 1 cup pecans and chocolate into remaining egg mixture; pour into pie crust. Stir caramel topping into reserved egg mixture; carefully pour over pecan filling.

3. Bake 50 to 55 minutes or until filling is set about 3 inches from edge. Cool completely on wire rack. Garnish with whipped cream and grated chocolate.

LEMON TART

MAKES 8 TO 10 SERVINGS

**Pastry for Single-Crust Pie
(page 44)**
- 5 **eggs**
- 1 **tablespoon cornstarch**
- 1 **cup sugar**
- ½ **cup (1 stick) butter**
- ½ **cup fresh lemon juice**

1. Prepare pie pastry. Preheat oven to 450°F.

2. Roll out pastry on floured surface into 11-inch circle. Line 9-inch tart pan with removable bottom with pastry, pressing onto bottom and up side. Trim excess crust. Prick bottom and side of crust with fork. Bake 9 to 10 minutes or until golden brown. Cool completely. *Reduce oven temperature to 350°F.*

3. Meanwhile, attach wire whip to stand mixer. Whip eggs and cornstarch in mixer bowl until well blended. Combine sugar, butter and lemon juice in small saucepan; cook and stir over medium-low heat just until butter melts. With mixer running on low speed, add sugar mixture in thin, steady stream. Return mixture to saucepan; cook over medium heat 8 to 10 minutes or until thickened, stirring constantly. (Do not boil.) Pour into medium bowl; stir 1 minute or until cooled slightly. Let cool 10 minutes. Pour into crust.

4. Bake 25 to 30 minutes or until set. Cool completely on wire rack. Cut into wedges.

STRAWBERRY–RHUBARB PIE

MAKES 8 SERVINGS

Pastry for Double-Crust Pie (page 43)

1½ **cups sugar**

½ **cup cornstarch**

2 **tablespoons quick-cooking tapioca**

1 **tablespoon grated lemon peel**

¼ **teaspoon ground allspice**

4 **cups sliced rhubarb (1-inch pieces)**

3 **cups sliced fresh strawberries**

1 **egg, lightly beaten**

1. Prepare pie pastry. Preheat oven to 425°F. Roll out one pastry disc into 11-inch circle on floured surface. Line 9-inch pie plate with pastry.

2. Combine sugar, cornstarch, tapioca, lemon peel and allspice in large bowl. Add rhubarb and strawberries; toss to coat. Pour into crust.

3. Roll out remaining pastry disc into 10-inch circle; cut into ½-inch-wide strips. Arrange in lattice design over fruit. Seal and flute edge. Brush pastry with egg.

4. Bake 50 minutes or until filling is thick and bubbly and crust is golden brown. Cool on wire rack. Serve warm or at room temperature.

FRESH FRUIT TART

MAKES 8 SERVINGS

1⅔ cups all-purpose flour

⅓ cup sugar

¼ teaspoon salt

½ cup (1 stick) butter, softened and cut into pieces

1 egg yolk

2 to 3 tablespoons milk

1 package (8 ounces) cream cheese, softened

⅓ cup strawberry jam

2 to 3 cups mixed assorted fresh fruit, such as sliced kiwi, blueberries, sliced peaches, sliced plums, raspberries and halved strawberries

¼ cup apple jelly, melted

1. Attach flat beater to stand mixer. Combine flour, sugar and salt in mixer bowl. Add butter; mix on low speed until mixture resembles coarse crumbs. Add egg yolk and 2 tablespoons milk; mix on low speed until dough leaves side of bowl. Add additional milk by teaspoons, if necessary. Shape dough into a disc. Wrap in plastic wrap and refrigerate 30 minutes or until firm.

2. Preheat oven to 350°F. Roll dough out on lightly floured surface to ¼-inch thickness. Cut 12-inch circle; transfer to 10-inch tart pan with removable bottom. Press lightly onto bottom and up side of pan; trim edges even with edge of pan. Bake 16 to 18 minutes or until light golden brown. Transfer to wire rack; cool completely.

3. Beat cream cheese and jam in mixer bowl on medium speed until well blended. Spread evenly over cooled crust. Arrange fruit decoratively over cream cheese layer. Brush fruit with apple jelly. Serve immediately or refrigerate up to 2 hours before serving.

MAPLE PECAN TART

MAKES 8 SERVINGS

Pastry for Single-Crust Pie (page 44)

1¼ cups (5 ounces) pecan halves

¾ cup sugar

2 eggs

⅓ cup corn syrup

⅓ cup maple syrup

2 tablespoons butter, melted

2 tablespoons bourbon or whiskey (optional)

1 teaspoon vanilla

1. Prepare pie pastry. Preheat oven to 350°F. Roll pastry into 11-inch circle on lightly floured surface. Press onto bottom and up side of 9-inch tart pan with removable bottom. Trim edge. Arrange pecans in single layer on pastry.

2. Attach wire whip to stand mixer. Whip sugar and eggs in mixer bowl on medium speed until well blended. Add corn syrup, maple syrup, butter, bourbon, if desired, and vanilla; mix until well blended. Pour mixture evenly over pecans. (Pecans will rise to the surface during baking.)

3. Bake 30 minutes or until golden brown and center is set. Cool completely in pan on wire rack.

LATTICE–TOPPED CHERRY PIE

MAKES 8 SERVINGS

Pastry for Double-Crust Pie (page 43)

- 6 **cups pitted sweet Bing cherries**
- ¾ **cup granulated sugar**
- 3 **tablespoons plus 1 teaspoon cornstarch**
- 2 **tablespoons lemon juice**

Half-and-half

Sanding sugar or additional granulated sugar

1. Prepare pie pastry. Preheat oven to 400°F.

2. Combine cherries, granulated sugar, cornstarch and lemon juice in large bowl; toss to coat. Let stand 15 minutes or until syrup forms.

3. Roll out one pastry disc into 11-inch circle on floured surface. Line 9-inch pie plate with pastry, allowing excess to drape over edge. Roll out remaining pastry disc into 11-inch circle; cut into 12 to 14 strips about ½ inch wide.

4. Pour filling into crust. Arrange pastry strips in lattice design over fruit. Tuck ends of strips under edge of bottom crust; seal edge. Brush crust with half-and-half; sprinkle with sanding sugar. Cover loosely with foil.

5. Bake 30 minutes. Remove foil; bake 30 minutes or until filling is thick and bubbly and crust is golden brown. Cool on wire rack.

LEMON MERINGUE PIE

MAKES 8 SERVINGS

Pastry for Single-Crust Pie (page 44)

FILLING

- 1½ cups water
- 1 cup sugar
- ⅓ cup cornstarch
- ¼ teaspoon salt
- 4 egg yolks, lightly beaten
- ½ cup fresh lemon juice (3 to 4 lemons), strained
- 2 tablespoons grated lemon peel
- 2 tablespoons butter

MERINGUE

- 1 tablespoon cornstarch
- ⅓ cup water
- 6 tablespoons sugar, divided
- ½ teaspoon vanilla
- 4 egg whites
- ¼ teaspoon cream of tartar

1. Prepare pie pastry. Roll out pastry into 11-inch circle on floured surface. Line 9-inch pie plate with pastry; flute edge. Refrigerate 15 minutes. Preheat oven to 350°F.

2. For filling, combine 1½ cups water, 1 cup sugar, ⅓ cup cornstarch and salt in medium saucepan. Bring to a simmer over medium heat; cook and stir until sugar dissolves and mixture thickens.

3. Whisk in egg yolks in thin, steady stream. Whisk in lemon juice, lemon peel and butter. Return to a simmer; cook 1 minute. Pour into prepared crust.

4. For meringue, stir 1 tablespoon cornstarch into ⅓ cup water in small saucepan until smooth. Stir in 1 tablespoon sugar and vanilla. Cook over low heat until thick paste forms, stirring frequently. Remove from heat; cool slightly.

5. Attach wire whip to stand mixer. Beat egg whites in mixer bowl on high speed until foamy. Gradually add remaining 5 tablespoons sugar and cream of tartar; whip until soft peaks form. Add cornstarch mixture, 1 tablespoon at a time, whipping until stiff peaks form.

6. Spread meringue over filling. Bake 12 to 15 minutes or until peaks and swirls of meringue are golden brown. Cool completely on wire rack.

COUNTRY PECAN PIE

MAKES 8 SERVINGS

Pastry for Single-Crust Pie (page 44)

1¼ cups dark corn syrup

4 eggs

½ cup packed brown sugar

¼ cup (½ stick) butter, melted

2 teaspoons all-purpose flour

1½ teaspoons vanilla

1½ cups pecan halves

1. Prepare pie pastry. Roll out pastry into 11-inch circle on floured surface. Line 9-inch pie plate with pastry; flute edge. Refrigerate 15 minutes. Preheat oven to 350°F.

2. Attach flat beater to stand mixer. Beat corn syrup, eggs, brown sugar and butter in mixer bowl on medium speed 2 to 3 minutes or until well blended. Stir in flour and vanilla until blended. Pour into pie crust. Arrange pecans on top.

3. Bake 40 to 45 minutes or until center is puffed and golden brown. Cool completely on wire rack.

SWEDISH APPLE PIE

MAKES 8 TO 10 SERVINGS

4   **Granny Smith apples, peeled and sliced**

1   **cup plus 1 tablespoon sugar, divided**

1   **tablespoon ground cinnamon**

¾   **cup (1½ sticks) butter, melted**

1   **cup all-purpose flour**

1   **egg**

½   **cup chopped nuts**

½   **teaspoon salt**

1. Preheat oven to 350°F.

2. Spread apples in 9-inch deep-dish pie plate or 9-inch square baking dish. Combine 1 tablespoon sugar and cinnamon in small bowl; sprinkle over apples and drizzle with butter.

3. Attach flat beater to stand mixer. Beat remaining 1 cup sugar, flour, egg, nuts and salt in mixer bowl just until blended. (Mixture will be thick.) Spread batter over apples.

4. Bake 50 to 55 minutes or until top is golden brown. Cool completely on wire rack.

ITALIAN CHOCOLATE PIE ALLA LUCIA

MAKES 8 SERVINGS

Pastry for Single-Crust Pie (page 44)

¼ cup pine nuts

3 tablespoons packed brown sugar

1 tablespoon grated orange peel

4 ounces bittersweet chocolate, coarsely chopped

3 tablespoons butter

1 can (5 ounces) evaporated milk

3 eggs

3 tablespoons hazelnut liqueur

1 teaspoon vanilla

Sweetened whipped cream (recipe follows)

Chocolate curls (recipe follows)

1. Prepare pie pastry. Roll out pastry into 11-inch circle on floured surface. Line 9-inch pie plate with pastry; flute edge. Refrigerate 15 minutes.

2. Toast pine nuts in dry nonstick skillet over medium heat, stirring constantly until golden brown and aromatic. Remove from heat. Finely chop when cool enough to handle.

3. Combine pine nuts, brown sugar and orange peel in small bowl. Sprinkle onto bottom of pie crust; gently press into crust.

4. Preheat oven to 325°F. Cook chocolate and butter in small saucepan over low heat, stirring constantly until melted and smooth. Cool to room temperature.

5. Attach flat beater to stand mixer. Beat chocolate mixture and evaporated milk in mixer bowl on medium speed until blended. Add eggs, one at a time, beating well after each addition. Stir in hazelnut liqueur and vanilla. Pour into crust.

6. Bake 30 to 40 minutes or until set. Cool completely on wire rack. Refrigerate until ready to serve. Serve with whipped cream and chocolate curls, if desired.

Sweetened Whipped Cream: Attach wire whip to stand mixer. Whip 1 cup heavy cream, 2 tablespoons powdered sugar and ½ teaspoon vanilla in chilled mixer bowl on high speed until soft peaks form.

Chocolate Curls: Melt ½ cup semisweet chocolate chips and 1 teaspoon vegetable oil in a medium microwavable bowl on MEDIUM (50%) 1 minute. Stir well. Spread chocolate mixture in 2-inch-wide ribbon shapes on piece of parchment paper. Let set for 1 minute; then, using the edge of a spatula, lift and scrape chocolate into curls. Place curls on a parchment paper-lined baking sheet. Let stand until set or refrigerate until ready to use.

PRALINE PUMPKIN TART

MAKES 8 SERVINGS

1¼ cups all-purpose flour

1 tablespoon granulated sugar

¾ teaspoon salt, divided

¼ cup shortening

¼ cup (½ stick) cold butter, cut into small pieces

3 to 4 tablespoons cold water

1 can (15 ounces) solid-pack pumpkin

1 can (12 ounces) evaporated milk

1 cup packed brown sugar, divided

2 eggs

1 teaspoon ground cinnamon

½ teaspoon ground ginger

¼ teaspoon ground cloves

⅓ cup chopped pecans

⅓ cup quick oats

1 tablespoon butter, softened

1. Attach flat beater to stand mixer. Combine flour, granulated sugar and ¼ teaspoon salt in mixer bowl. Add shortening and cold butter; mix on low speed 1 minute or until coarse crumbs form.

2. With mixer running on low speed, drizzle in enough water just until dough starts to come together. Turn out dough onto lightly floured surface; press into a ball. Wrap in plastic wrap. Refrigerate about 1 hour or until chilled.

3. Roll out dough on lightly floured surface into circle 1 inch larger than 11×7-inch baking dish. Transfer dough to baking dish; cover with plastic wrap and refrigerate 30 minutes.

4. Preheat oven to 400°F. Pierce crust with tines of fork at ¼-inch intervals. Line baking dish with foil; fill with dried beans, uncooked rice or ceramic pie weights. Bake 10 minutes or until set. Remove from oven; gently remove foil lining and beans. Bake 5 minutes or until golden brown. Cool completely on wire rack.

5. Meanwhile, beat pumpkin, evaporated milk, ⅔ cup brown sugar, eggs, cinnamon, remaining ½ teaspoon salt, ginger and cloves in mixer bowl on low speed until well blended. Pour into prepared crust. Bake 35 minutes.

6. Meanwhile for topping, combine remaining ⅓ cup brown sugar, pecans, oats and softened butter in mixer bowl. Mix on low speed until coarse crumbs form. Sprinkle topping over center of tart, leaving 1½-inch rim around edge. Bake 15 minutes or until knife inserted 1 inch from center comes out clean. Cool completely on wire rack.

CAKES AND CUPCAKES

CARAMEL–TOPPED CREAM CAKE

MAKES 12 TO 16 SERVINGS

3 cups cake flour
2½ teaspoons baking powder
½ teaspoon salt
1 cup (2 sticks) butter
2 cups granulated sugar
4 eggs
1 cup milk
1 teaspoon vanilla
½ teaspoon almond extract
Caramel Topping (recipe follows)
Buttery Frosting (recipe follows)
½ cup chopped walnuts or pecans

1. Preheat oven to 350°F. Grease and flour three 9-inch round cake pans. Sift flour, baking powder and salt into medium bowl.

2. Attach flat beater to stand mixer. Beat butter and sugar in mixer bowl on medium-high speed until light and fluffy. Add eggs, one at a time, beating well after each addition. With mixer running on low speed, add flour mixture alternately with milk, beating well after each addition. Stir in vanilla and almond extract. Pour evenly into prepared pans.

3. Bake 20 to 25 minutes or until toothpick inserted into centers comes out clean. Cool in pans on wire racks 10 minutes. Loosen edges; invert onto racks to cool completely.

4. Prepare Caramel Topping and Buttery Frosting. Fill cake layers with three fourths of topping; frost top and side of cake with frosting. Drizzle with remaining topping; sprinkle with nuts.

CARAMEL TOPPING

3 cups granulated sugar, divided
¾ cup milk
½ cup (1 stick) butter, softened
1 egg, beaten
½ teaspoon vanilla
¼ teaspoon salt

1. Place ½ cup sugar in large heavy saucepan. Cook over medium heat without stirring until sugar is light golden brown. Stir in remaining 2½ cups sugar, milk, butter, egg, vanilla and salt.

2. Cook over medium heat 15 to 20 minutes or until candy thermometer registers 230°F, stirring occasionally; cool 5 minutes. Stir with wooden spoon until well blended and thickened.

BUTTERY FROSTING

½ cup (1 stick) butter, softened
3 cups sifted powdered sugar
2 tablespoons heavy cream
½ teaspoon vanilla

1. Beat butter in mixer bowl at medium speed 30 seconds or until creamy.

2. Gradually add powdered sugar alternately with cream; add vanilla. Beat on medium-high speed until light and fluffy.

CHOCOLATE CAKE

MAKES 12 TO 16 SERVINGS

2 cups all-purpose flour

1⅓ cups sugar

⅓ cup unsweetened cocoa powder

1 teaspoon baking powder

½ teaspoon baking soda

½ teaspoon salt

1 cup milk

½ cup (1 stick) butter

1 teaspoon vanilla

2 eggs

4 ounces unsweetened chocolate, melted

½ cup hot water

Ganache Frosting (recipe follows)

Chocolate curls (page 58)

1. Preheat oven to 350°F. Grease and flour ten 6-inch ramekins or two 8- or 9-inch pans.

2. Attach flat beater to stand mixer. Combine flour, sugar, cocoa, baking powder, baking soda and salt in mixer bowl. Add milk, butter and vanilla; beat on medium-low speed 1 minute. Add eggs and chocolate; beat on medium speed 2 minutes. Stir in water on low speed. Pour batter into prepared pans.

3. Bake individual cakes about 25 minutes or layer cakes 30 to 35 minutes or until toothpick inserted into centers comes out clean. Cool in pans on wire racks 10 minutes. Remove from pans; cool completely on wire racks.

4. Prepare Ganache Frosting Swirl over tops of cooled cakes; garnish with chocolate curls.

Chocolate Layer Cake: Bake cake in layer pans as above. Prepare Chocolate Buttercream Frosting (page 70); fill and frost cake. Prepare Ganache Frosting; pour evenly over cake and spread to coat. Garnish with chocolate curls.

GANACHE FROSTING

1¼ cups heavy cream

2 tablespoons butter

10 ounces bittersweet chocolate, chopped

1½ teaspoons vanilla

1. Bring cream and butter to a simmer in medium saucepan over medium heat. Add chocolate; remove from heat and let stand 5 minutes.

2. Add vanilla; whisk until smooth. Let stand until thickened but pourable.

MARBLED PUMPKIN CHEESECAKE

MAKES 12 TO 15 SERVINGS

Gingersnap Cookie Crust
(recipe follows)

4 packages (8 ounces each)
cream cheese, softened

½ cup sugar

6 eggs

1 cup sour cream

1 cup canned pumpkin puree

2 tablespoons all-purpose
flour

2 teaspoons ground
cinnamon

½ teaspoon ground ginger

½ teaspoon ground allspice

3 ounces semisweet
chocolate, melted

1. Prepare Gingersnap Cookie Crust.

2. *Increase oven temperature to 425°F.* Attach flat beater to stand mixer. Beat cream cheese in mixer bowl on medium-high speed about 3 minutes or until light and fluffy. Add sugar; beat until well blended. Add eggs, one at a time, beating well after each addition. Add sour cream, pumpkin, flour, cinnamon, ginger and allspice; beat until well blended.

3. Pour 2 cups batter into small bowl; stir in melted chocolate until well blended. Pour remaining batter into prepared crust. Spoon chocolate batter in large swirls over pumpkin batter in crust; draw knife through mixture to marbleize.

4. Bake 15 minutes. *Reduce oven temperature to 300°F.* Bake 45 minutes (center of cheesecake will not be set). Turn off oven; let cheesecake stand in oven with door slightly ajar 1 hour. Cool to room temperature in pan on wire rack. Cover and refrigerate overnight.

5. Remove side of pan from cheesecake; place cheesecake on serving plate.

GINGERSNAP COOKIE CRUST

1 cup gingersnap cookie
crumbs

½ cup graham cracker crumbs

¼ cup sugar

½ cup (1 stick) butter, melted

1. Preheat oven to 350°F. Combine cookie crumbs, cracker crumbs and sugar in small bowl. Mix in butter.

2. Press mixture evenly on bottom and 1 inch up side of 9-inch springform pan.

3. Bake 8 minutes; cool on wire rack.

GINGER STOUT CAKE

MAKES 12 TO 16 SERVINGS

2 cups all-purpose flour

2 teaspoons ground ginger

1½ teaspoons baking powder

1½ teaspoons baking soda

¾ teaspoon ground cinnamon

½ teaspoon salt

¼ teaspoon ground cloves

½ cup (1 stick) butter, softened

1 tablespoon grated fresh ginger *or* 1 teaspoon ground ginger

1 cup granulated sugar

½ cup packed brown sugar

3 eggs

1 bottle (11 ounces) Irish stout

½ cup molasses

Sweetened Whipped Cream (page 58, optional)

1. Preheat oven to 350°F. Grease 13×9-inch baking pan. Combine flour, ground ginger, baking powder, baking soda, cinnamon, salt and cloves in medium bowl.

2. Attach flat beater to stand mixer. Beat butter and grated ginger in mixer bowl on medium speed until creamy. Add granulated sugar and brown sugar; beat until light and fluffy. Add eggs, one at a time, beating well after each addition. Stir in molasses until well blended. Add flour mixture alternately with stout, beating well after each addition. Pour batter into prepared pan.

3. Bake 45 minutes or until toothpick inserted into center comes out clean. Cool completely in pan on wire rack. Garnish with whipped cream.

BLUEBERRY CRUMB CAKE

MAKES 12 TO 16 SERVINGS

1 cup chopped walnuts or pecans

2½ cups all-purpose flour, divided

1⅓ cups sugar, divided

¼ cup (½ stick) butter, softened

½ teaspoon ground cinnamon

1 tablespoon baking powder

1 teaspoon salt

½ teaspoon baking soda

1 cup milk

½ cup (1 stick) butter, melted

2 eggs

2 tablespoons lemon juice

2 cups fresh or thawed frozen
   blueberries

1. Preheat oven to 375°F. Grease 13×9-inch baking pan.

2. For topping, combine walnuts, ½ cup flour, ⅔ cup sugar, softened butter and cinnamon in large bowl until mixture forms coarse crumbs.

3. Whisk remaining 2 cups flour, ⅔ cup sugar, baking powder, salt and baking soda into another large bowl. Attach flat beater to stand mixer. Beat milk, melted butter, eggs and lemon juice in mixer bowl on medium-low speed or until well blended. Stir in flour mixture on low speed until blended. Pour batter into prepared pan. Sprinkle blueberries evenly over batter; sprinkle with topping.

4. Bake 40 to 45 minutes or until toothpick inserted into center comes out clean. Serve warm.

CHOCOLATE ESPRESSO CAKE

MAKES 12 TO 16 SERVINGS

2 cups cake flour

1½ teaspoons baking soda

½ teaspoon salt

½ cup (1 stick) butter, softened

1 cup granulated sugar

1 cup packed brown sugar

3 eggs

4 ounces unsweetened chocolate, melted

¾ cup sour cream

1 teaspoon vanilla

1 cup brewed espresso*

Espresso Chocolate Frosting (recipe follows)

Use fresh brewed espresso, instant espresso powder prepared according to directions on jar or 1 tablespoon instant coffee powder dissolved in 1 cup hot water.

1. Preheat oven to 350°F. Line bottoms of two 9-inch round cake pans with parchment paper; grease paper. Combine flour, baking soda and salt in medium bowl.

2. Attach flat beater to stand mixer. Beat butter and sugars in mixer bowl on medium speed until light and fluffy. Add eggs, one at a time, beating well after each addition. Add melted chocolate, sour cream and vanilla; beat until blended. Add flour mixture alternately with espresso, beating well on low speed after each addition. Pour batter evenly into prepared pans.

3. Bake 35 minutes or until toothpick inserted into centers comes out clean. Cool in pans on wire racks 10 minutes. Loosen edges and invert layers onto racks; cool completely.

4. Prepare Espresso Chocolate Frosting. Place one layer on cake plate; frost top. Place second layer over frosting. Frost top and side.

ESPRESSO CHOCOLATE FROSTING

½ cup (1 stick) butter, softened

4 cups powdered sugar

5 to 6 tablespoons brewed espresso, divided

½ cup semisweet chocolate chips, melted

1 teaspoon vanilla

Dash salt

1. Attach flat beater to stand mixer. Beat butter in mixer bowl on medium speed until creamy. Gradually add powdered sugar and 4 tablespoons espresso; beat on medium-low speed 3 minutes or until smooth.

2. Beat in melted chocolate, vanilla and salt on medium-high speed 4 minutes or until very light and fluffy, adding additional espresso, if needed.

Chocolate Buttercream Frosting: Add 2 tablespoons unsweetened cocoa powder with powdered sugar. Replace espresso with heavy cream.

CHERRY PINK CUPCAKES

MAKES 12 CUPCAKES

1 jar (10 ounces) maraschino
   cherries with stems

1¼ cups all-purpose flour

1½ teaspoons baking powder

½ teaspoon salt

1 cup granulated sugar

2 eggs

½ cup vegetable oil

½ cup milk

1 teaspoon vanilla

   **Cherry Pink Frosting
   (recipe follows)**

1. Preheat oven to 350°F. Line 12 standard (2½-inch) muffin cups with paper baking cups. Drain cherries, reserving juice for Cherry Pink Frosting. Reserve 12 cherries for garnish; stem and chop remaining cherries and squeeze out excess moisture. Spread cherries on paper towels to drain. Set aside.

2. Combine flour, baking powder and salt in medium bowl. Attach flat beater to stand mixer. Beat sugar and eggs in mixer bowl on medium speed until light and fluffy. Beat in flour mixture on low speed. Add oil, milk and vanilla; beat 1 minute or until smooth. Stir in chopped cherries. Pour batter evenly into prepared muffin cups.

3. Bake 20 to 23 minutes or until lightly browned and centers spring back when gently touched. Cool in pan on wire rack 5 minutes. Remove from pan; cool completely.

4. Meanwhile, prepare Cherry Pink Frosting. Fit piping bag with large star tip; fill with frosting. Pipe swirls of frosting on cupcakes. Garnish with reserved cherries.

CHERRY PINK FROSTING

1 cup (2 sticks) butter,
   softened

4 cups powdered sugar

2½ tablespoons reserved
   maraschino cherry juice

   Dash salt

1. Attach flat beater to stand mixer. Beat butter in mixer bowl on medium speed until creamy. Gradually add powdered sugar; beat until blended.

2. Add cherry juice and salt; beat on medium-high speed until fluffy. Add additional powdered sugar if needed for desired consistency.

ORANGE–ALMOND POUND CAKE

MAKES 2 LOAVES

- 3 cups all-purpose flour
- ½ teaspoon baking powder
- ½ teaspoon baking soda
- ½ teaspoon salt
- 1 cup milk
- 1 tablespoon orange juice
- 1 cup (2 sticks) butter, softened
- 2 cups sugar
- 2 eggs
- ½ teaspoon almond extract
- 1 teaspoon vanilla
- Fresh fruit and grated orange peel (optional)

1. Preheat oven to 350°F. Grease and flour two 9×5-inch loaf pans. Whisk flour, baking powder, baking soda and salt in medium bowl. Combine milk and orange juice in small bowl.

2. Attach flat beater to stand mixer. Beat butter and sugar in mixer bowl on medium speed until light and fluffy. Add eggs, one at a time, beating well after each addition. Beat in almond extract and vanilla. Add flour mixture alternately with milk mixture, beating well after each addition. Pour into prepared pans.

3. Bake 35 minutes or until toothpick inserted into centers comes out clean. Cool in pans 10 minutes. Remove to wire racks; cool completely. Garnish with fruit and orange peel.

BANANA CAKE

MAKES 12 TO 16 SERVINGS

2½ cups all-purpose flour
1 tablespoon baking soda
½ teaspoon salt
1 cup granulated sugar
¾ cup packed brown sugar
½ cup (1 stick) butter, softened
2 eggs
1 teaspoon vanilla
3 ripe bananas, mashed (about 1⅔ cups)
⅔ cup buttermilk
   Chocolate Buttercream Frosting
   (page 70)

1. Preheat oven to 350°F. Grease two 8-inch round cake pans. Whisk flour, baking soda and salt in medium bowl.

2. Attach flat beater to stand mixer. Beat granulated sugar, brown sugar and butter in mixer bowl on medium speed until well blended. Add eggs and vanilla; beat until blended. Stir in bananas. Alternately add flour mixture and buttermilk, beating until well blended after each addition. Pour batter into prepared pans.

3. Bake 35 minutes or until toothpick inserted into centers comes out clean. Cool in pans 10 minutes. Remove to wire racks; cool completely. Prepare frosting; fill and frost cake.

CLASSIC YELLOW CAKE

MAKES 8 TO 10 SERVINGS

2 cups all-purpose flour

4 teaspoons baking powder

½ teaspoon salt

1½ cups sugar

½ cup (1 stick) butter, softened

1 cup milk

1 teaspoon vanilla

3 eggs

Creamy White Frosting (recipe follows)

1. Preheat oven to 350°F. Grease and flour cake pan(s) or grease and line with waxed paper.

2. Attach flat beater to stand mixer. Sift flour, baking powder and salt in large bowl. Stir in sugar. Add butter, milk and vanilla; beat on low speed 30 seconds. Beat on medium speed 2 minutes. Add eggs; beat 2 minutes. Pour into prepared cake pan(s) and bake as directed below until toothpick inserted into centers comes out clean.

3. Bake one 13×9-inch cake 28 to 35 minutes; one 10-inch bundt cake 45 to 55 minutes; two 9-inch cakes 25 to 30 minutes; two 8-inch squares 25 to 30 minutes; three 8-inch rounds 20 to 25 minutes; eight large 4-inch cupcakes 35 to 40 minutes; or 24 standard (2¾-inch) cupcakes 18 to 20 minutes.

4. Cool in pans on wire rack 10 minutes. Loosen edge from pan; invert onto rack, remove waxed paper and cool completely.

5. Prepare Creamy White Frosting. Fill and frost cake with frosting.

CREAMY WHITE FROSTING

1 cup milk

3 tablespoons all-purpose flour

1 cup (2 sticks) butter, softened

1 cup powdered sugar

1 teaspoon vanilla

1. Whisk milk into flour in medium saucepan. Bring to a boil over medium heat, whisking frequently. Cook and stir 1 to 2 minutes or until thickened. Cool to room temperature.

2. Attach flat beater to stand mixer. Beat butter in mixer bowl on medium speed until creamy. Add powdered sugar; beat until fluffy. Add flour mixture and vanilla; beat until thick and smooth.

CHOCOLATE HAZELNUT DELIGHT

MAKES 16 SERVINGS

CAKE

- 1 package (2¼ ounces) chopped hazelnuts
- 2 cups cake flour
- ½ cup unsweetened cocoa powder
- 1½ teaspoons baking soda
- 1 teaspoon baking powder
- 1 teaspoon salt
- 1 cup (2 sticks) butter, softened
- 1 cup packed brown sugar
- ½ cup granulated sugar
- 3 eggs
- 4 ounces unsweetened chocolate, melted
- 1 teaspoon vanilla
- 1 cup milk
- ½ cup warm water

FROSTING

- 1 cup (2 sticks) butter, softened
- 4 cups powdered sugar
- ¼ cup milk
- 1 teaspoon vanilla
- 1 jar (13 ounces) chocolate hazelnut spread
- 16 whole toasted hazelnuts (optional)

1. For cake, preheat oven to 350°F. Spray three 9-inch round cake pans with nonstick cooking spray. Line bottoms with parchment paper.

2. Spread chopped hazelnuts on baking sheet. Bake 7 minutes or until lightly browned and fragrant. Place on clean kitchen towel; rub hazelnuts with towel to remove skins. Finely chop.

3. Whisk flour, cocoa, baking soda, baking powder and salt in medium bowl until well blended. Stir in chopped hazelnuts.

4. Attach flat beater to stand mixer. Beat 1 cup butter, brown sugar and granulated sugar in mixer bowl on medium-high speed about 5 minutes or until light and fluffy. Add eggs, one at a time, beating well after each addition. Beat in melted chocolate and 1 teaspoon vanilla. Add flour mixture alternately with milk, mixing well after each addition. Stir in warm water. Pour batter evenly into prepared pans.

5. Bake 30 minutes or until toothpick inserted into centers comes out clean. Cool in pans on wire racks 10 minutes. Invert onto wire racks; peel off parchment. Cool completely on wire rack.

6. For frosting, attach flat beater to stand mixer. Place 1 cup butter in mixer bowl; beat on medium-high speed until creamy. Beat in powdered sugar until light and fluffy. Stir in ¼ cup milk and 1 teaspoon vanilla. Add chocolate hazelnut spread; beat until smooth.

7. Place one cake layer on serving plate; spread with frosting. Repeat with remaining layers. Frost top and side of cake. Pipe 16 rosettes around cake and top each with one whole hazelnut, if desired.

PORTER CAKE

MAKES 10 SERVINGS

3½ cups all-purpose flour

1½ teaspoons pumpkin pie spice

1 teaspoon baking powder

½ teaspoon salt

1 cup (2 sticks) butter

1 bottle (10 ounces) porter or stout

1 cup packed brown sugar

1½ cups golden raisins

1½ cups raisins

Finely grated peel of 1 orange

2 eggs

¼ chopped candied citrus peel

¼ cup candied cherries

1. Preheat oven to 350°F. Grease 9-inch springform pan; line bottom with parchment paper. Grease parchment paper; dust bottom and side of pan with flour, tapping out excess. Line baking sheet with foil.

2. Attach flat beater to stand mixer. Combine flour, pumpkin pie spice, baking powder and salt in bowl of stand mixer. Combine butter, porter and brown sugar in large saucepan; cook over medium heat about 7 minutes or until butter is melted and sugar is dissolved, stirring occasionally. Remove from heat; stir in raisins and orange peel. Let cool about 15 minutes or until just warm.

3. Add porter mixture and eggs to flour mixture; mix on low speed just until combined. Stir in candied citrus peel and cherries. Pour batter into prepared pan; place on prepared baking sheet.

4. Bake 60 to 65 minutes or until toothpick inserted into center comes out clean. Cool in pan on wire rack 15 minutes. Remove side of pan; cool completely on wire rack.

CRANBERRY POUND CAKE

MAKES 12 SERVINGS

1½ cups sugar
1 cup (2 sticks) butter, softened
¼ teaspoon salt
¼ teaspoon ground mace
4 eggs
2 cups cake flour
1 cup chopped fresh or frozen cranberries

1. Preheat oven to 350°F. Grease and flour 9×5-inch loaf pan.

2. Attach flat beater to stand mixer. Beat sugar, butter, salt and mace in mixer bowl on medium speed until light and fluffy. Add eggs, one at a time, beating until well blended after each addition. Add flour, ½ cup at a time, beating well on low speed after each addition. Fold in cranberries. Spoon batter into prepared pan.

3. Bake 60 to 70 minutes or until toothpick inserted into center comes out clean. Cool in pan on wire rack 5 minutes. Run knife around edges of pan to loosen cake; cool 30 minutes. Remove from pan; cool completely on wire rack.

DESSERTS

WARM APPLE AND BLUEBERRY CRISP

MAKES 6 SERVINGS

6 apples, peeled and sliced

2 cups fresh or frozen
blueberries

½ cup packed brown sugar,
divided

¼ cup orange juice

½ cup all-purpose flour

½ cup old-fashioned oats

¼ cup (½ stick) cold butter,
cut into small pieces

½ teaspoon baking powder

¼ teaspoon baking soda

¼ teaspoon ground cinnamon

¼ teaspoon ground ginger

1. Preheat oven to 375°F. Grease 9-inch square baking pan.

2. Combine apples, blueberries, ¼ cup brown sugar and orange juice in medium bowl; toss to coat. Spoon into prepared pan.

3. Attach flat beater to stand mixer. Combine flour, oats, remaining ¼ cup brown sugar, butter, baking powder, baking soda, cinnamon and ginger in mixer bowl; mix on low speed until coarse crumbs form. Sprinkle over fruit mixture.

4. Bake 45 minutes or until apples are tender and topping is golden brown.

CHOCOLATE–RASPBERRY BREAD PUDDING

MAKES 6 TO 8 SERVINGS

8 slices hearty bread, cut
  into ½-inch cubes

¼ cup (½ stick) butter, melted

2 cups milk

4 eggs

¾ cup sugar

1 teaspoon vanilla

½ cup fresh raspberries

½ cup bittersweet or
  semisweet chocolate
  chips

1. Grease 9-inch baking dish. Combine bread cubes and butter in prepared dish; toss to coat.

2. Attach wire whip to stand mixer. Whip milk, eggs, sugar and vanilla in mixer bowl on medium-low speed until well blended. Pour over bread cubes. Cover and refrigerate 2 hours.

3. Preheat oven to 350°F. Sprinkle raspberries and chocolate chips evenly over bread mixture.

4. Bake 40 to 50 minutes or until golden brown and center is set. Let stand 10 minutes before serving.

STRAWBERRY–RHUBARB CRISP

MAKES 8 SERVINGS

- 4 cups sliced rhubarb (1-inch pieces)
- 3 cups sliced strawberries (about 1 pint)
- ¾ cup granulated sugar
- ⅓ cup plus ¼ cup all-purpose flour, divided
- 1 tablespoon grated lemon peel
- 1 cup old-fashioned oats
- ½ cup packed brown sugar
- 1 teaspoon ground cinnamon
- ½ teaspoon salt
- ⅓ cup butter, melted

1. Preheat oven to 375°F. Combine rhubarb and strawberries in large bowl. Combine granulated sugar, ¼ cup flour and lemon peel in small bowl. Sprinkle over fruit; toss to coat. Pour into 9-inch square baking pan.

2. Attach flat beater to stand mixer. Combine oats, brown sugar, remaining ⅓ cup flour, cinnamon and salt in mixer bowl. Stir in butter on low speed until mixture is crumbly. Sprinkle over rhubarb mixture.

3. Bake 45 to 50 minutes or until filling is bubbly and topping is lightly browned. Serve warm or at room temperature.

MINI STRAWBERRY SHORTCAKES

MAKES 16 SERVINGS

1 quart fresh strawberries,
   hulled and sliced

½ cup sugar, divided

1 cup all-purpose flour

2 teaspoons baking powder

¼ teaspoon salt

¼ cup (½ stick) cold butter,
   cut into small pieces

1¼ cups heavy cream, divided

1. Combine strawberries and ¼ cup sugar in medium bowl; set aside.

2. Preheat oven to 425°F. Attach flat beater to stand mixer. Combine flour, 2 tablespoons sugar, baking powder and salt in mixer bowl. Add butter; mix on low speed until mixture resembles coarse crumbs. Gradually add ½ cup cream, mixing on low speed until dough comes together. (Dough will be slightly sticky.)

3. Turn out dough onto lightly floured surface; knead gently 4 to 6 times. Pat dough into 6-inch square. Cut into 16 (1½-inch) squares with sharp knife. Place 2 inches apart on ungreased baking sheet.

4. Bake about 10 minutes or until golden brown. Remove to wire rack to cool slightly.

5. Meanwhile, attach wire whip to stand mixer. Whip remaining ¾ cup cream and 2 tablespoons sugar in mixer bowl on high speed until soft peaks form.

6. Split biscuits in half horizontally. Fill with berry mixture and whipped cream.

CHOCOLATE CRÈME BRÛLÉE

MAKES 4 SERVINGS

- 2 **cups heavy whipping cream**
- 3 **ounces semisweet or bittersweet chocolate, finely chopped**
- 3 **egg yolks**
- ¼ **cup granulated sugar**
- 2 **teaspoons vanilla**
- 3 **tablespoons packed brown sugar**

1. Preheat oven to 325°F. Heat cream in medium saucepan over medium heat just until bubbles begin to form around edge of saucepan. *Do not boil*. Remove from heat; stir in chocolate until melted and smooth. Set aside to cool slightly.

2. Attach flat beater to stand mixer. Beat egg yolks and granulated sugar in mixer bowl on medium-high speed 5 minutes or until thick and pale yellow. Beat in chocolate mixture and vanilla until blended.

3. Divide mixture among four 6-ounce custard cups or individual baking dishes. Place cups in baking pan; place pan in oven. Pour boiling water into baking pan to reach halfway up sides of custard cups. Cover pan loosely with foil.

4. Bake 30 minutes or just until edges are set. Transfer cups to wire rack; cool completely. Wrap with plastic wrap and refrigerate 4 hours or up to 3 days.

5. Preheat broiler. Spread about 2 teaspoons brown sugar evenly over each cup. Broil 3 to 4 minutes or until sugar bubbles and browns, watching carefully. Serve immediately.

CHERRY–ALMOND CLAFOUTI

MAKES 4 SERVINGS

- ½ **cup slivered almonds, toasted***
- ½ **cup powdered sugar**
- ⅔ **cup all-purpose flour**
- ⅔ **cup granulated sugar**
- ¼ **teaspoon salt**
- ½ **cup (1 stick) melted butter**
- ⅔ **cup milk**
- 2 **eggs**
- ½ **teaspoon vanilla**
- 1 **cup fresh cherries, pitted and quartered or fresh raspberries**

To toast almonds, spread in single layer on baking sheet. Bake in preheated 350°F oven 8 to 10 minutes or until golden brown, stirring frequently.

1. Preheat oven to 350°F. Grease four 6-ounce ramekins; place on baking sheet.

2. Process almonds in food processor until coarsely ground. Add powdered sugar; pulse until well blended. Add flour, granulated sugar and salt. Pulse until well blended. Attach wire whip to stand mixer. Transfer almond mixture to mixer bowl.

3. With mixer running on medium speed, drizzle in butter in thin, steady stream. Gradually add milk, eggs and vanilla; mix until blended. Gently stir in cherries.

4. Divide batter among prepared ramekins. Bake about 50 minutes or until tops and sides are puffy and golden. Let cool 5 to 10 minutes before serving.

CHOCOLATE PEANUT BUTTER DOUGHNUTS

MAKES 18 TO 20 DOUGHNUTS

DOUGHNUTS

- 1½ cups all-purpose flour
- 2 tablespoons cornstarch
- ¾ teaspoon baking powder
- ½ teaspoon salt
- ¼ teaspoon baking soda
- ¼ teaspoon ground nutmeg
- ½ cup granulated sugar
- 1 egg
- ¼ cup (½ stick) butter, melted
- 2 ounces bittersweet chocolate, melted
- ½ teaspoon vanilla
- ¼ cup buttermilk

FILLING

- ¼ cup (½ stick) butter, softened
- 6 tablespoons creamy peanut butter
- 2 cups powdered sugar
- ⅛ teaspoon salt*
- 3 tablespoons heavy whipping cream
- ¼ cup bittersweet chocolate chips, melted
- ¼ cup chopped peanuts

Taste filling before adding salt; some peanut butter may not need additional salt.

1. Whisk flour, cornstarch, baking powder, salt, baking soda and nutmeg in large bowl.

2. Attach flat beater to stand mixer. Beat granulated sugar and eggs in mixer bowl on high speed 3 minutes or until pale and thick. Stir in melted butter, 2 ounces melted chocolate and vanilla on medium speed. Add flour mixture alternately with buttermilk, mixing on low speed after each addition. Press plastic wrap directly onto surface of dough. Refrigerate at least 1 hour.

3. Pour about 2 inches of oil into Dutch oven or large heavy saucepan; clip deep-fry or candy thermometer to side of pot. Heat over medium-high heat to 365°F to 375°F. Line large wire rack with paper towels.

4. Meanwhile, generously flour work surface. Turn out dough onto work surface. Dust top with flour and roll dough about ¼-inch thick; cut out circles with 2-inch biscuit cutter. Gather and reroll scraps. Line large wire rack with paper towels.

5. Working in batches, add donuts to hot oil. Cook 2 minutes, turning twice. Do not crowd pan and adjust heat to maintain temperature during frying. Drain on prepared rack.

6. For filling, beat ¼ cup butter and peanut butter in mixer bowl on medium speed until smooth. Add powdered sugar and salt, if desired; beat on medium speed until well blended. Add cream; beat on high speed 3 minutes or until very light and fluffy.

7. Place filling in pastry bag fitted with large star tip. Cut rounded tops off of donuts; pipe swirls of filling onto donuts and replace tops. Drizzle with melted chocolate and sprinkle with peanuts.

BLUEBERRY SHORTCAKE

MAKES 4 SERVINGS

SHORTCAKE

- **1 cup all-purpose flour**
- **2 tablespoons sugar**
- **2 teaspoons baking powder**
- **¼ teaspoon salt**
- **¼ cup (½ stick) cold butter, cut into pieces**
- **6 to 8 tablespoons milk**

FILLING

- **2 cups fresh blueberries***
- **3 tablespoons sugar**
- **Grated peel of 1 small lemon**
- **1 tablespoon fresh lemon juice**
- **2 tablespoons water**

TOPPING

- **⅔ cup heavy cream**
- **1 tablespoon sugar**

Or use 2 cups thawed frozen blueberries and reduce the water to 1 tablespoon.

1. Preheat oven to 425°F.

2. For shortcake, attach flat beater to stand mixer. Combine flour, 2 tablespoons sugar, baking powder and salt in mixer bowl. Add butter; mix on low speed about 1 minute or until mixture resembles coarse crumbs. Add milk by tablespoons, stirring just until dough comes together (dough will be slightly sticky).

3. Divide dough into four pieces. Shape into 2½-inch rounds, about 1 inch high. Place on ungreased baking sheet. Bake 15 minutes or until golden brown. Remove to wire rack; cool completely.

4. For filling, combine blueberries, 3 tablespoons sugar, lemon peel, lemon juice and water in small saucepan. Bring to a boil over high heat. Reduce heat; cover and simmer 10 minutes or until berries are tender and sauce has thickened, stirring occasionally.

5. For topping, attach wire whip to stand mixer. Whip cream and 1 tablespoon sugar in mixer bowl on medium-high speed until stiff peaks form.

6. Split biscuits in half. Spoon about ¼ cup filling on bottom halves; replace tops. Garnish with whipped cream.

PLUM–RHUBARB CRUMBLE

MAKES 6 TO 8 SERVINGS

1½ pounds plums, pitted and cut into wedges (4 cups)

1½ pounds rhubarb, cut into ½-inch pieces (5 cups)

1 cup granulated sugar

1 teaspoon finely grated fresh ginger

¼ teaspoon ground nutmeg

3 tablespoons cornstarch

¾ cup old-fashioned oats

½ cup all-purpose flour

½ cup packed brown sugar

¼ teaspoon salt

½ cup sliced almonds, toasted*

½ cup (1 stick) cold butter, cut into small pieces

*To toast almonds, spread in single layer on ungreased baking sheet. Bake in preheated 350°F oven 5 minutes or until golden brown, stirring frequently.

1. Combine plums, rhubarb, granulated sugar, ginger and nutmeg in large bowl; toss to coat. Cover and let stand at room temperature 2 hours.

2. Preheat oven to 375°F. Grease 9-inch round or square baking dish.

3. Pour juices from fruit into small saucepan; bring to a boil over medium-high heat. Cook about 12 minutes or until reduced to syrupy consistency, stirring occasionally. Stir in cornstarch until well blended. Stir into fruit; pour into prepared baking dish.

4. Attach flat beater to stand mixer. Combine oats, flour, brown sugar and salt in mixer bowl. Add butter; mix on low speed until mixture is clumpy. Stir in almonds. Sprinkle evenly over fruit mixture. Place baking dish on baking sheet.

5. Bake about 50 minutes or until filling is bubbly and topping is golden brown. Cool 1 hour before serving.

ENGLISH BREAD PUDDING

MAKES 6 TO 8 SERVINGS

14 slices day-old firm white bread (about 12 ounces), crusts trimmed

1½ cups milk

⅓ cup butter, softened

⅓ cup packed brown sugar

1 teaspoon ground cinnamon

¼ teaspoon ground nutmeg

¼ teaspoon ground cloves

1 medium apple, peeled and chopped

1 package (6 ounces) mixed dried fruit, chopped

1 egg

⅓ cup chopped nuts

Sweetened whipped cream (page 58)

1. Tear bread into pieces; place in bowl of stand mixer. Pour milk over bread; let soak 30 minutes.

2. Preheat oven to 350°F. Spray 9×5-inch loaf pan with nonstick cooking spray.

3. Attach flat beater to stand mixer. Add butter, brown sugar, cinnamon, nutmeg and cloves to bowl with bread mixture; beat on low speed about 1 minute or until smooth. Add apple, dried fruit and egg; beat until blended. Stir in nuts. Pour into prepared pan.

4. Bake 1 hour 15 minutes to 1 hour 30 minutes or until toothpick inserted into center comes out clean. Cool in pan 10 minutes; remove to wire rack to cool slightly. Serve warm with whipped cream.

CRUNCH PEACH COBBLER

MAKES 6 TO 8 SERVINGS

⅓ cup plus 1 tablespoon granulated sugar, divided

1 tablespoon cornstarch

¾ cup peach juice or nectar

½ teaspoon vanilla

2 cups all-purpose flour, divided

½ cup packed brown sugar

⅓ cup old-fashioned oats

¼ cup (½ stick) butter, melted

½ teaspoon ground cinnamon

½ teaspoon salt

½ cup (1 stick) cold butter, cut into pieces

4 to 5 tablespoons cold water

2 pounds fresh peaches, peeled and sliced

Sweetened whipped cream (page 58, optional)

1. For sauce, combine ⅓ cup granulated sugar and cornstarch in small saucepan. Slowly whisk in peach juice. Cook over low heat until thickened, whisking constantly. Remove from heat; stir in vanilla.

2. For topping, combine ½ cup flour, brown sugar, oats, melted butter and cinnamon in small bowl; stir until mixture forms coarse crumbs. Set aside.

3. Preheat oven to 350°F. Attach flat beater to stand mixer. Combine remaining 1½ cups flour, 1 tablespoon granulated sugar and salt in mixer bowl. Add cold butter, mix on low speed until mixture resembles coarse crumbs. With mixer running on low speed, add water 1 tablespoon at a time until mixture holds together. Press together to form a ball.

4. Roll out dough into 10-inch square, ⅛-inch thick, on lightly floured surface. Press dough onto bottom and about 1 inch up sides of 8-inch square baking dish; trim edges. Arrange peaches over crust; pour peach sauce over peaches. Sprinkle with crumb topping.

5. Bake 45 minutes or until topping is golden brown. Serve warm or at room temperature with whipped cream, if desired.

BREADS AND BEYOND

YEAST BREADS...100

QUICK BREADS.. 122

MUFFINS, SCONES AND DOUGHNUTS 138

COFFEECAKES AND BRUNCH BREADS 158

SWEET AND SAVORY SNACKS 174

YEAST BREADS

SPANIKOPITA PULL–APARTS

MAKES 24 ROLLS

3 cups all-purpose flour

1 package (¼ ounce) rapid-rise active dry yeast

1½ teaspoons salt

1 cup warm water (120°F)

2 tablespoons olive oil

4 tablespoons (½ stick) butter, melted, divided

1 package (10 ounces) frozen chopped spinach, thawed and squeezed dry

4 green onions, finely chopped (about ¼ cup packed)

1 clove garlic, minced

1 teaspoon dried dill weed

½ teaspoon salt

⅛ teaspoon freshly ground black pepper

1 cup (4 ounces) crumbled feta cheese

¾ cup (3 ounces) grated Monterey Jack cheese, divided

1. Attach dough hook to stand mixer. Combine flour, yeast and salt in mixer bowl. Stir in water and olive oil with wooden spoon to form rough dough. Knead on low speed 5 to 7 minutes or until dough is smooth and elastic.

2. Shape dough into a ball. Place in large lightly greased bowl; turn once to grease surface. Cover and let rise in warm place 30 to 45 minutes or until doubled in size.

3. Brush large (10-inch) ovenproof skillet with ½ tablespoon butter. Turn out dough onto lightly floured surface. Divide into 24 pieces; roll into balls.

4. Combine spinach, green onions, garlic, dill, salt and pepper in medium bowl; mix well to break apart spinach. Add feta, ½ cup Monterey Jack and remaining 3½ tablespoons butter; mix well.

5. Coat each ball of dough with spinach mixture; arrange in single layer in prepared skillet. Sprinkle any remaining spinach mixture between and over dough. Cover and let rise in warm place about 40 minutes or until almost doubled in size.

6. Preheat oven to 350°F. Sprinkle remaining ¼ cup Monterey Jack over dough.

7. Bake 35 to 40 minutes or until golden brown. Serve warm.

PRETZEL ROLLS

MAKES 12 ROLLS

1¼ cups lager or pale ale, at
   room temperature

3 tablespoons packed brown
   sugar

2 tablespoons milk

2 tablespoons butter, melted

1 package (¼ ounce) rapid-
   rise active dry yeast

3 to 4 cups bread flour,
   divided

2 teaspoons salt

4 quarts water

½ cup baking soda

2 teaspoons kosher salt or
   pretzel salt

1. Attach flat beater to stand mixer. Stir lager, brown sugar, milk, butter and yeast in mixer bowl. Add 1 cup flour and salt. Mix on low speed, adding enough flour to make stiff dough that cleans the bowl. Replace flat beater with dough hook. Knead on medium-low speed 8 minutes or until smooth and slightly tacky, adding additional flour as needed. Shape dough into a ball. Place in large lightly greased bowl; turn once to grease surface. Cover and let rise in warm place 1 hour or until doubled in size.

2. Turn out dough onto lightly floured surface; knead briefly. Divide into 12 equal pieces. Shape each piece into a smooth ball by gently pulling top surface to underside; pinch bottom to seal. Place on ungreased baking sheet. Cover and let rise in warm place 30 minutes or until doubled in size.

3. Preheat oven to 425°F. Grease second baking sheet or line with parchment paper.

4. Bring water and baking soda to a boil in large saucepan. Add rolls to water, a few at a time; cook until puffed, turning once. Drain on clean kitchen towel. Place rolls on prepared baking sheet 2 inches apart. Cut 1½-inch-wide X in top of each roll using kitchen shears. Sprinkle with kosher salt.

5. Bake 15 to 18 minutes or until crisp and brown. Remove from baking sheet; cool on wire rack.

EGG BAGELS

MAKES 12 BAGELS

½ to ¾ cup warm water (105° to 115°F), divided

1 package (¼ ounce) active dry yeast

2 tablespoons plus 1 teaspoon sugar, divided

2½ cups all-purpose flour

2 eggs

1 tablespoon canola oil

1 teaspoon salt

2 quarts water

2 tablespoons sugar

2 tablespoons cold water

1. Attach flat beater to stand mixer. Combine ¼ cup warm water, yeast and 1 teaspoon sugar in mixer bowl; stir to dissolve yeast. Let stand 5 minutes or until bubbly.

2. Add 2 cups flour, 1 egg, oil, salt and ¼ cup warm water; mix on low speed 1 minute or until soft dough forms. Replace flat beater with dough hook. Knead on low speed 5 to 7 minutes or until dough is smooth and elastic, adding additional flour 1 tablespoon at a time to prevent sticking, if needed.

3. Shape dough into a ball. Place in large lightly greased bowl; turn once to grease surface. Cover and let stand in warm place 15 minutes.

4. Grease baking sheet. Turn out dough onto lightly floured surface. Divide dough into 12 pieces. Roll each piece into 6-inch-long rope; shape into rings and pinch ends to seal. Place on prepared baking sheet; let stand 15 minutes.

5. Preheat oven to 425°F. Combine 8 cups water and remaining 2 tablespoons sugar in large saucepan or Dutch oven; bring to a boil over medium-high heat. Working in batches, gently place bagels in boiling water; cook 1 minute, turning once. Remove bagels from water using slotted spoon; place on same baking sheet.

6. Beat remaining egg and 2 tablespoons cold water in small bowl. Brush evenly over bagels.

7. Bake 20 to 25 minutes or until golden brown. Remove to wire racks; cool completely.

CINNAMON ROLLS

MAKES 24 ROLLS

DOUGH

- ¼ cup warm water (115° to 120°F)
- 1 package (¼ ounce) active dry yeast
- ½ cup milk
- ¼ cup granulated sugar
- 2 tablespoons butter, melted and cooled
- 1 egg
- 1 teaspoon vanilla
- ½ teaspoon salt
- 2½ to 2¾ cups all-purpose flour, divided

FILLING

- ⅓ cup granulated sugar
- 1 tablespoon grated orange peel (optional)
- 1 teaspoon ground cinnamon
- 2 tablespoons butter, melted

GLAZE

- ¾ cup powdered sugar
- 1 to 2 tablespoons milk or orange juice

1. For dough, attach flat beater to stand mixer. Combine water and yeast in mixer bowl; stir to dissolve yeast. Let stand 5 minutes.

2. Whisk milk, ¼ cup granulated sugar, 2 tablespoons butter, egg, vanilla and salt in medium bowl; add to yeast mixture. Add 2½ cups flour; stir until soft dough forms. Replace flat beater with dough hook. Knead on low speed 5 to 7 minutes or until dough is smooth and elastic, adding additional flour 1 tablespoon at a time to prevent dough from sticking, if needed.

3. Shape dough into a ball. Place in large lightly greased bowl; turn once to grease surface. Cover and let rise in warm place about 1 hour or until doubled in size.

4. For filling, combine ⅓ cup granulated sugar, orange peel, if desired, and cinnamon in small bowl. Grease two 8-inch round cake pans. Divide dough in half. Working with half at a time, roll out dough into 12×8-inch rectangle on lightly floured surface. Brush with 1 tablespoon melted butter; sprinkle with half of filling mixture. Beginning with long side, tightly roll up dough; cut into 12 (1-inch) slices. Arrange slices, cut sides up, in one pan. Repeat with remaining dough, 1 tablespoon butter and filling. Cover and let rise in warm place about 1 hour or until doubled in size.

5. Preheat oven to 350°F. Bake 18 to 20 minutes or until rolls are golden brown. Cool in pans on wire racks 5 minutes.

6. For glaze, whisk powdered sugar and milk in small bowl until blended. Add additional milk, if necessary, to reach desired consistency. Drizzle glaze over warm rolls.

CARDAMOM ROLLS

MAKES 12 ROLLS

DOUGH

- ½ cup water
- ½ cup milk
- 1 tablespoon active dry yeast
- ½ cup plus 1 teaspoon granulated sugar, divided
- ½ cup (1 stick) butter, softened
- 3 eggs
- ½ teaspoon vanilla
- 4 cups all-purpose flour
- ¾ teaspoon salt

FILLING

- ¼ cup (½ stick) butter, very soft
- ¼ cup packed brown sugar
- 1½ teaspoons ground cardamom
- 1 teaspoon ground cinnamon
- 1 tablespoon butter, melted
- Pearl sugar (optional)

1. Heat water and milk in small saucepan to about 115°F. Transfer to small bowl; stir in yeast and 1 teaspoon granulated sugar. Let stand 5 minutes or until mixture is bubbly.

2. Attach flat beater to stand mixer. Beat butter and remaining ½ cup granulated sugar in mixer bowl on medium speed until light and fluffy. Add eggs, one at a time, beating well after each addition. Beat in vanilla. Reduce speed to low; beat in yeast mixture, 2 cups flour and salt. Beat at medium speed 2 minutes.

3. Replace flat beater with dough hook. Add remaining 2 cups flour. Knead on low speed until most of flour is incorporated. Beat on medium speed 3 minutes (dough will be sticky). Cover and let rise in warm place about 1½ hours or until doubled. Stir down dough. Cover and refrigerate 2 hours or overnight.

4. Roll out dough on floured surface into 18-inch square. Spread 2 tablespoons butter over top half of dough. Sprinkle with brown sugar, cardamom and cinnamon. Fold bottom of dough over filling; pinch ends to seal. Roll into 20×10-inch rectangle. Cut dough into 12 strips. Cut each strip lengthwise into two or three pieces, leaving them connected at the top. Holding uncut end, wrap cut dough around fingers and pull into knot shape, turning to expose some of filling. Place on baking sheet. Brush with melted butter; sprinkle with pearl sugar. Let stand 15 minutes.

5. Preheat oven to 375°F. Bake 15 to 20 minutes or until golden. Remove to wire rack to cool.

BANANA-PECAN SWIRL

MAKES 1 LOAF

DOUGH

- ½ cup milk
- 3 cups bread flour, divided
- ¼ cup granulated sugar
- 1 package (¼ ounce) active dry yeast
- 1 teaspoon salt
- ½ teaspoon ground cinnamon
- 2 tablespoons butter, melted
- ½ cup mashed banana (about 1 small)
- 1 egg

FILLING

- ½ cup packed brown sugar
- ¼ cup (½ stick) butter, softened
- 1 teaspoon ground cinnamon
- ½ cup chopped pecans

TOPPING

- ½ cup powdered sugar
- 1½ teaspoons milk
- ¼ teaspoon ground cinnamon
- 2 tablespoons chopped pecans

1. For dough, heat ½ cup milk in small saucepan to about 120°F. Attach flat beater to stand mixer. Combine 1 cup flour, granulated sugar, yeast, salt and ½ teaspoon cinnamon in bowl of stand mixer. Add milk and melted butter; mix on medium speed 1 minute. Add banana and egg; mix 1 minute or until well blended.

2. Replace flat beater with dough hook. Add remaining 2 cups flour; knead on low speed 5 to 7 minutes or until dough is smooth and elastic. Shape dough into a ball. Place in large lightly greased bowl; turn once to grease surface. Cover and let rise in warm place 1 hour or until doubled in size.

3. Grease baking sheet. Turn out dough onto lightly floured surface. Roll into 14×12-inch rectangle; transfer to prepared baking sheet.

4. For filling, combine brown sugar, softened butter and 1 teaspoon cinnamon in small bowl. Spread mixture over dough; sprinkle with ½ cup pecans. Starting from long end, tightly roll up, pinching ends to seal. Shape roll into "S" with top and bottom ends folded under. Cover and let rise in warm place 45 minutes or until doubled in size.

5. Preheat oven to 325°F. Bake 35 to 40 minutes or until golden brown and loaf sounds hollow when tapped. Remove to wire rack to cool.

6. For topping, combine powdered sugar, 1½ teaspoons milk and ¼ teaspoon cinnamon in medium bowl until smooth. Drizzle over bread; sprinkle with 2 tablespoons pecans.

BAGELS

MAKES 6 OR 9 BAGELS

- 2 teaspoons rapid-rise active dry yeast
- 4 tablespoons sugar, divided
- 1½ cups warm water (115° to 120°F), divided
- 4 cups bread flour
- 2 teaspoons salt
- 3 quarts water
- 2 to 3 tablespoons cornmeal
- 1 egg, beaten
- 1 to 2 tablespoons sesame seeds, poppy seeds or caraway seeds (optional)

1. Stir yeast and 1 tablespoon sugar into ½ cup warm water in small bowl until yeast is dissolved. Let stand 5 minutes or until bubbly.

2. Attach dough hook to stand mixer. Combine 2 cups flour, 2 tablespoons sugar and salt in mixer bowl. Stir in remaining 1 cup warm water and yeast mixture with wooden spoon until rough dough forms. Add remaining 2 cups flour. Knead on low speed 5 to 7 minutes or until dough is smooth and elastic.

3. Shape dough into ball. Place in large lightly greased bowl; turn once to grease surface. Cover and let rise in warm place about 1 hour or until doubled in size.

4. Turn out dough onto floured surface; knead briefly. Cut into 6 or 9 pieces; shape into balls. Place on floured surface; let rest 10 minutes. Poke thumb through center of each ball to make hole. Stretch into ring shapes. Place on floured surface. Let stand, uncovered, 15 minutes or until puffy. (Do not overproof bagels.)

5. Meanwhile, preheat oven to 400°F. Bring 3 quarts water and remaining 1 tablespoon sugar to a boil in large saucepan. Grease two baking sheets; sprinkle with cornmeal.

6. Cook 3 bagels at a time in boiling water 5 minutes, turning often. Remove bagels using slotted spoon; drain briefly on paper towels. Place 2 inches apart on prepared baking sheets. Brush with beaten egg and sprinkle with desired toppings. Bake 25 to 30 minutes or until golden brown. Remove to wire racks to cool.

NO–KNEAD SANDWICH BREAD

MAKES 1 LOAF

2 packages (¼ ounce each)
  active dry yeast

¾ cup warm water (110° to
  115°F)

1 cup all-purpose flour

⅔ cup old-fashioned oats

¼ cup soy flour

¼ cup wheat gluten

¼ cup sesame seeds

2 teaspoons sugar

1 teaspoon salt

1. Stir yeast into water in small bowl until yeast is dissolved. Let stand 5 minutes or until bubbly.

2. Attach flat beater to stand mixer. Combine all-purpose flour, oats, soy flour, gluten, sesame seeds, sugar and salt in mixer bowl. With mixer running on medium speed, pour in yeast mixture in thin steady stream; mix just until dough forms a ball. Cover bowl around flat beater with towel; let dough rise 1 hour or until doubled.

3. Grease 8×4-inch loaf pan. Remove towel from top of bowl. Mix on medium speed just until dough forms a ball. Turn out onto lightly floured surface. Shape into disc. (Dough will be slightly sticky.) Roll dough on floured surface into 12×8-inch rectangle. Roll up from short side; fold under ends and place in prepared pan. Cover and let rise in warm place 45 minutes or until doubled in size.

4. Preheat oven to 375°F. Bake 35 minutes or until bread is golden brown and sounds hollow when tapped. Remove from pan and cool completely on wire rack.

PESTO PULL–APART SWIRLS

MAKES 24 SERVINGS

- 3 **cups all-purpose flour**
- 1 **package (¼ ounce) rapid-rise active dry yeast**
- 1½ **teaspoons salt**
- 1 **cup warm water (120°F)**
- 2 **tablespoons plus 1 teaspoon olive oil, divided**
- 5 **tablespoons shredded Parmesan cheese, divided**
- 1 **jar (4½ ounces) pesto sauce (about ¼ cup)**

1. Attach dough hook to stand mixer. Combine flour, yeast and salt in mixer bowl. Stir in water and 2 tablespoons oil with wooden spoon to form rough dough. Knead on low speed 5 to 7 minutes or until dough is smooth and elastic.

2. Shape dough into a ball. Place in large lightly greased bowl; turn once to grease surface. Cover and let rise in warm place 45 minutes or until doubled in size.

3. Brush bottom and side of 8-inch round pan with remaining 1 teaspoon oil; sprinkle with 2 tablespoons cheese. Turn out dough onto lightly floured surface; roll into 20×12-inch rectangle. Spread pesto over dough. Starting with long side, tightly roll up dough, pinching seam to seal. Stretch or roll dough until 24 inches in length. Cut crosswise into 1-inch slices. Place 12 slices cut sides up in prepared pan; sprinkle with 2 tablespoons cheese. Top with remaining 12 slices; sprinkle with remaining 1 tablespoon cheese. Cover and let rise in warm place 30 minutes.

4. Preheat oven to 350°F. Bake 20 minutes or until lightly browned. Invert onto wire rack; invert again onto serving plate. Serve warm.

ANADAMA BREAD

MAKES 2 LOAVES

2 cups water

½ cup yellow cornmeal

¼ cup (½ stick) butter, cut into pieces

½ cup molasses

5½ to 6 cups all-purpose flour, divided

1 package (¼ ounce) active dry yeast

1 teaspoon salt

1. Attach flat beater to stand mixer. Bring water to a boil in medium saucepan. Whisk in cornmeal; cook 1 minute, whisking constantly. Reduce heat to low; whisk in butter. Cook 3 minutes, stirring frequently. Transfer to mixer bowl. Add molasses; mix on low until well blended. Let stand 15 to 20 minutes to cool (to about 90°F), mixing on low speed occasionally.

2. Stir in 2 cups flour, yeast and salt on low speed until rough dough forms and cleans side of bowl. Replace flat beater with dough hook. Knead on low speed 5 to 7 minutes, adding remaining flour, ½ cup at a time until dough cleans side of bowl.

3. Shape dough into a ball. Place in large lightly greased bowl; turn once to grease surface. Cover and let rise in warm place about 1 hour or until doubled in size.

4. Punch down dough. Knead dough on well-floured surface 1 minute. Cut dough in half. Cover with towel; let rest 10 minutes.

5. Grease two loaf pans. Shape dough into loaves and place in pans. Cover and let rise in warm place about 30 minutes or until doubled in size.

6. Preheat oven to 350°F. Bake 30 to 35 minutes or until loaves are browned and sound hollow when tapped. Immediately remove from pans; cool on wire racks.

CINNAMON RAISIN BREAD

MAKES 2 LOAVES

¼ cup (½ stick) butter

1 cup plus 2 tablespoons
  milk

2 tablespoons honey

4 cups all-purpose flour

2½ teaspoons salt

2½ teaspoons active dry yeast

2 eggs

1 cup raisins

2 tablespoons melted butter,
  divided

3 tablespoons sugar

4 teaspoons ground
  cinnamon

1. Melt ¼ cup butter in small saucepan over low heat. Stir in milk and honey; cook until mixture is about 115°F. Whisk in eggs; remove from heat.

2. Attach dough hook to stand mixer. Combine flour, salt and yeast in mixer bowl. Add egg mixture and raisins; knead on low speed until dough forms a ball and cleans side of bowl. Continue kneading 2 minutes.

3. Place dough in large lightly greased bowl; turn once to grease surface. Cover and let rise in warm place 1 to 1½ hours or until dough is doubled in size.

4. Grease and flour two 8×4-inch loaf pans. Punch down dough; cut in half. Shape each half into 8×10-inch rectangle. Brush 1 tablespoon melted butter over rectangles.

5. Combine sugar and cinnamon in small bowl. Reserve 2 teaspoons cinnamon-sugar; sprinkle remaining cinnamon-sugar evenly over dough.

6. Starting from short sides, tightly roll up dough; place in prepared pans. Cover and let rise in warm place 1 to 1½ hours or until almost doubled in size.

7. Preheat oven to 375°F. Bake loaves 35 minutes or until golden brown (internal temperature should register 180°F), rotating pans once. Brush tops with remaining 1 tablespoon melted butter; sprinkle with reserved cinnamon-sugar. Cool in pans 10 minutes. Remove to wire rack; cool completely.

CRUNCHY WHOLE GRAIN BREAD

MAKES 2 LOAVES

2 cups warm water (105° to 115°F), divided

⅓ cup honey

2 tablespoons vegetable oil

1 tablespoon salt

2 packages (¼ ounce each) active dry yeast

2 to 2½ cups whole wheat flour, divided

1 cup bread flour

1¼ cups old-fashioned oats, divided

½ cup sunflower kernels

½ cup assorted grains and seeds*

1 egg white

1 tablespoon water

Try a combination of uncooked millet, barley, chia seeds, flaxseed and pumpkin seeds.

1. Combine 1½ cups warm water, honey, oil and salt in small saucepan. Cook and stir over low heat until warm (115° to 120°F).

2. Attach dough hook to stand mixer. Dissolve yeast in remaining ½ cup water in mixer bowl. Let stand 5 minutes. Stir in honey mixture. Add 1 cup whole wheat flour and bread flour; knead on low speed 2 minutes or until combined. Gradually stir in 1 cup oats, sunflower kernels and assorted grains. Add remaining whole wheat flour, ½ cup at a time, just until dough begins to form a ball. Continue kneading 7 to 10 minutes or until dough is smooth and elastic.

3. Shape dough into a ball. Place in large lightly greased bowl; turn once to grease surface. Cover and let rise in warm place 1½ to 2 hours or until doubled in size.

4. Grease two 9×5-inch loaf pans. Punch down dough. Divide in half. Shape each half into loaf; place in prepared pans. Cover and let rise in warm place 1 hour or until almost doubled in size.

5. Preheat oven to 375°F. Whisk egg white and 1 tablespoon water in small bowl; brush over tops of loaves. Sprinkle with remaining ¼ cup oats. Bake 35 to 45 minutes or until loaves sound hollow when tapped. Cool in pans 10 minutes. Remove to wire racks; cool completely.

QUICK BREADS

CRANBERRY PUMPKIN NUT BREAD

MAKES 1 LOAF

- 2 **cups all-purpose flour**
- 2 **teaspoons pumpkin pie spice**
- 1 **teaspoon baking powder**
- ½ **teaspoon baking soda**
- ½ **teaspoon salt**
- 1 **cup canned pumpkin puree**
- ¾ **cup granulated sugar**
- ½ **cup packed brown sugar**
- 2 **eggs**
- ⅓ **cup vegetable or canola oil**
- 1 **cup chopped dried cranberries**
- ¾ **cup chopped macadamia nuts, toasted***

To toast macadamia nuts, spread on baking sheet. Bake in 350°F oven 8 to 10 minutes or until lightly browned, stirring occasionally. Immediately remove from pan; cool completely before using.

1. Preheat oven to 350°F. Grease 9×5-inch loaf pan.

2. Attach flat beater to stand mixer. Combine flour, pumpkin pie spice, baking powder, baking soda and salt in mixer bowl.

3. Combine pumpkin, granulated sugar, brown sugar, eggs and oil in medium bowl; whisk until well blended. Add to flour mixture; mix on medium-low speed just until dry ingredients are moistened. Stir in cranberries and nuts. Pour batter into prepared pan.

4. Bake 45 to 50 minutes or until toothpick inserted into center comes out clean. Cool in pan 15 minutes. Remove to wire rack; cool completely.

LOADED BANANA BREAD

MAKES 1 LOAF

6 tablespoons (¾ stick) butter, softened

⅓ cup granulated sugar

⅓ cup packed brown sugar

2 eggs

3 ripe bananas, mashed

½ teaspoon vanilla

1½ cups all-purpose flour

2½ teaspoons baking powder

¼ teaspoon salt

1 can (8 ounces) crushed pineapple, drained

⅓ cup flaked coconut

¼ cup mini chocolate chips

⅓ cup chopped walnuts (optional)

1. Preheat oven to 350°F. Grease 9×5-inch loaf pan.

2. Attach flat beater to stand mixer. Beat butter, granulated sugar and brown sugar in mixer bowl on medium speed until light and fluffy. Beat in eggs, one at a time, mixing well after each addition. Add bananas and vanilla. Beat just until combined.

3. Sift flour, baking powder and salt in small bowl. Gradually add to banana mixture, mixing on low speed just until combined. Fold in pineapple, coconut and chocolate chips.

4. Spoon batter into prepared pan. Top with walnuts, if desired. Bake 50 minutes or until toothpick inserted into center comes out almost clean. Cool in pan 1 hour. Remove to wire rack; cool completely.

BLUEBERRY–APRICOT STREUSEL BREAD

MAKES 1 LOAF

- 2 cups plus 2 tablespoons all-purpose flour, divided
- 1 cup plus 2 tablespoons sugar, divided
- 1 teaspoon baking powder
- ½ teaspoon baking soda
- ½ teaspoon salt
- ¾ cup chopped dried apricots
- ¾ cup chopped dried blueberries
- ¾ cup buttermilk
- ½ cup (1 stick) butter, melted
- 1 egg
- 1 teaspoon vanilla
- 1 teaspoon almond extract
- 2 tablespoons chopped sliced almonds
- 1 teaspoon ground cinnamon
- 2 tablespoons cold butter, cut into small pieces
- Lemon curd (recipe follows, optional)

1. Preheat oven to 350°F. Grease 9×5-inch loaf pan.

2. Attach flat beater to stand mixer. Combine 2 cups flour, 1 cup sugar, baking powder, baking soda and salt in mixer bowl. Stir in apricots and blueberries.

3. Whisk buttermilk, melted butter, egg, vanilla and almond extract in medium bowl. Add to dry ingredients; mix on low speed just until moistened. Spread batter evenly in prepared pan.

4. For topping, combine remaining 2 tablespoons flour, 2 tablespoons sugar, almonds and cinnamon in small bowl. Cut in cold butter with fork or fingers until crumbly. Sprinkle evenly over batter.

5. Bake 55 to 65 minutes or until toothpick inserted into center comes out clean. Cool in pan 15 minutes. Remove to wire rack; cool completely. Serve with lemon curd, if desired.

LEMON CURD

MAKES ABOUT 1 CUP

- ½ cup sugar
- 6 tablespoons butter
- ⅓ cup fresh lemon juice
- ½ tablespoon grated lemon peel
- Pinch of salt
- 2 eggs, beaten

1. Combine sugar, butter, lemon juice, lemon peel and salt in medium saucepan over medium heat, stirring until butter is melted and sugar is dissolved. Gradually whisk in eggs in thin steady stream. Cook over medium-low heat 5 minutes or until thickened to the consistency of pudding, whisking constantly.

2. Strain through fine-mesh sieve into medium bowl. Press plastic wrap onto surface; refrigerate until cold.

DATE NUT BREAD

MAKES 1 LOAF

- **2 cups all-purpose flour**
- **½ cup packed brown sugar**
- **1 tablespoon baking powder**
- **½ teaspoon salt**
- **¼ cup (½ stick) cold butter, cut into pieces**
- **1 cup toasted chopped walnuts**
- **1 cup chopped dates**
- **1¼ cups milk**
- **1 egg**
- **½ teaspoon grated lemon peel**

1. Preheat oven to 375°F. Grease 9×5-inch loaf pan.

2. Attach flat beater to stand mixer. Combine flour, brown sugar, baking powder and salt in mixer bowl. Add butter; mix on low speed until mixture resembles fine crumbs. Stir in walnuts and dates.

3. Whisk milk, egg and lemon peel in small bowl. Add to flour mixture; stir just until moistened. Spread in prepared pan.

4. Bake 45 to 50 minutes or until toothpick inserted into center comes out clean. Cool in pan on wire rack 10 minutes. Remove to wire rack; cool completely.

ZUCCHINI BREAD

MAKES 1 LOAF

1 cup chopped pitted dates

1 cup water

1 cup whole wheat flour

1 cup all-purpose flour

2 tablespoons granulated sugar

1 teaspoon baking powder

½ teaspoon baking soda

½ teaspoon salt

½ teaspoon ground cinnamon

¼ teaspoon ground cloves

2 eggs

1 cup shredded zucchini, pressed dry
    with paper towels

1. Preheat oven to 350°F. Grease 8×4-inch loaf pan.

2. Combine dates and water in small saucepan; bring to a boil over medium-high heat. Remove from heat; let stand 15 minutes.

3. Attach flat beater to stand mixer. Combine flours, granulated sugar, baking powder, baking soda, salt and cloves in mixer bowl. Add eggs, date mixture and zucchini; mix on low speed just until moistened. Pour into prepared pan.

4. Bake 30 to 35 minutes or until toothpick inserted into center comes out clean. Cool 5 minutes. Remove to wire rack; cool completely.

CORN BREAD

MAKES 9 SERVINGS

1 cup all-purpose flour

1 cup yellow cornmeal

⅓ cup sugar

2 teaspoons baking powder

½ teaspoon salt

1 cup milk

⅓ cup vegetable oil

1 egg

2 jalapeño peppers, finely
   chopped (optional)

Honey Butter (recipe
   follows, optional)

1. Preheat oven to 400°F. Grease 8-inch square baking pan.

2. Attach flat beater to stand mixer. Combine flour, cornmeal, sugar, baking powder and salt in mixer bowl. Whisk milk, oil, egg and jalapeños, if desired, in small bowl until blended. Add to flour mixture; mix on low speed just until moistened. Spread batter evenly in prepared pan.

3. Bake 20 to 25 minutes or until golden brown and toothpick inserted in center comes out clean. Cut into squares. Serve warm with honey butter, if desired.

Corn Muffins: Spoon batter into 12 (2½-inch) greased or paper-lined muffin pan cups. Bake 20 minutes or until golden brown and toothpick inserted into centers comes out clean. Immediately remove from pan; cool on wire rack 10 minutes.

Honey Butter: Attach flat beater to stand mixer. Beat 6 tablespoons softened butter, 2 tablespoons honey and ¼ teaspoon salt in mixer bowl on medium speed until smooth.

BOSTON BLACK COFFEE BREAD

MAKES 1 LOAF

- ½ **cup rye flour**
- ½ **cup cornmeal**
- ½ **cup whole wheat flour**
- 1 **teaspoon baking soda**
- ½ **teaspoon salt**
- ¾ **cup strong brewed coffee, at room temperature**
- ⅓ **cup molasses**
- ¼ **cup canola oil**
- ¾ **cup raisins**

1. Preheat oven to 325°F. Grease and flour 9×5-inch loaf pan.

2. Attach flat beater to stand mixer. Combine rye flour, cornmeal, whole wheat flour, baking soda and salt in mixer bowl. Add coffee, molasses and oil; mix on low speed until blended. Fold in raisins. Pour batter into prepared pan.

3. Bake 50 minutes or until toothpick inserted into center comes out clean. Cool completely in pan on wire rack.

IRISH SODA BREAD

MAKES 12 SERVINGS

4 cups all-purpose flour

¼ cup sugar

1 tablespoon baking powder

1 teaspoon baking soda

1 teaspoon salt

1 tablespoon caraway seeds

½ cup (1 stick) cold butter, cut into pieces

1 cup currants or raisins

1¾ cups buttermilk

1 egg

1. Preheat oven to 350°F. Grease large baking sheet.

2. Attach flat beater to stand mixer. Sift flour, sugar, baking powder, baking soda and salt into mixer bowl. Stir in caraway seeds. Add butter; mix on low speed until mixture resembles coarse crumbs. Stir in currants. Whisk buttermilk and egg in medium bowl until well blended. Add to flour mixture; mix on low speed until mixture forms soft dough that clings together and forms a ball.

3. Turn out dough onto well-floured surface. Knead gently 10 to 12 times. Place dough on prepared baking sheet; pat into 7-inch round. Score top of dough with tip of sharp knife, making an "X" about 4 inches long and ¼ inch deep.

4. Bake 55 to 60 minutes or until toothpick inserted into center comes out clean. Immediately remove from baking sheet; cool on wire rack. Bread is best eaten the day it is made.

CITRUS BREAD

MAKES 1 LOAF

1¾ cups all-purpose flour

¾ cup sugar

1 tablespoon plus ½ teaspoon grated lemon peel, divided

2 teaspoons baking powder

1½ teaspoons grated orange peel

¼ teaspoon salt

1 cup milk

½ cup vegetable oil

1 egg, beaten

1 teaspoon vanilla

¼ cup orange marmalade

1. Preheat oven to 350°F. Grease and flour 9×5-inch loaf pan.

2. Attach flat beater to stand mixer. Combine flour, sugar, 1 tablespoon lemon peel, baking powder, orange peel and salt in mixer bowl. Whisk milk, oil, egg and vanilla in small bowl until well blended. Add to flour mixture; mix on low speed just until blended. (Batter will be thin.) Pour into prepared pan.

3. Bake 45 minutes or until toothpick inserted into center comes out clean. Cool bread in pan on wire rack 5 minutes.

4. Meanwhile, combine marmalade and remaining ½ teaspoon lemon peel in small microwavable bowl. Microwave on HIGH 15 seconds or until slightly melted. Remove bread from pan to wire rack; spread marmalade mixture evenly over top. Cool completely before serving.

RHUBARB BREAD

MAKES 1 LOAF

- 2 **cups all-purpose flour**
- 1 **cup sugar**
- 1 **tablespoon baking powder**
- 1 **teaspoon salt**
- ¼ **teaspoon ground cinnamon**
- 1 **cup milk**
- 2 **eggs**
- ⅓ **cup butter, melted**
- 2 **teaspoons grated fresh ginger (about 1 inch)**
- 10 **ounces chopped fresh rhubarb (¼-inch pieces, about 2¼ cups total)**
- ¾ **cup chopped walnuts, toasted***

*To toast walnuts, spread in single layer on ungreased baking sheet. Bake in preheated 350°F oven 6 to 8 minutes or until lightly browned, stirring frequently.

1. Preheat oven to 350°F. Grease 9×5-inch loaf pan.

2. Attach flat beater to stand mixer. Combine flour, sugar, baking powder, salt and cinnamon in mixer bowl.

3. Whisk milk, eggs, butter and ginger in medium bowl until well blended. Add to flour mixture; mix on low speed just until dry ingredients are moistened. Add rhubarb and walnuts; stir just until blended. Pour batter into prepared pan.

4. Bake 60 to 65 minutes or until toothpick inserted into center comes out clean. Cool in pan on wire rack 15 minutes. Remove to wire rack; cool completely.

BLUEBERRY PECAN TEA BREAD

MAKES 1 LOAF

2½ cups all-purpose flour

½ cup granulated sugar

½ cup packed brown sugar

2 teaspoons baking powder

1 teaspoon ground cinnamon

½ teaspoon baking soda

½ teaspoon salt

½ cup dried blueberries or cranberries

½ cup chopped pecans

1½ cups buttermilk*

2 eggs

¼ cup (½ stick) butter, melted

1 teaspoon vanilla

Or substitute 4½ teaspoons vinegar or lemon juice plus enough milk to equal 1½ cups. Let stand 5 minutes.

1. Preheat oven to 350°F. Grease 9×5-inch loaf pan.

2. Attach flat beater to stand mixer. Combine flour, granulated sugar, brown sugar, baking powder, cinnamon, baking soda and salt in mixer bowl. Stir in blueberries and pecans.

3. Whisk buttermilk, eggs, butter and vanilla in medium bowl. Add to flour mixture; mix on low speed just until dry ingredients are moistened. Pour batter into prepared pan.

4. Bake 40 to 45 minutes or until toothpick inserted into center comes out clean. Cool in pan on wire rack 10 minutes. Remove to wire rack; cool completely.

WHEAT GERM BREAD

MAKES 1 LOAF

¾ cup wheat germ, divided

¾ cup all-purpose flour

½ cup whole wheat flour

¼ cup packed brown sugar

1 teaspoon baking soda

½ teaspoon baking powder

¼ teaspoon salt

½ cup raisins

1 cup buttermilk

¼ cup (½ stick) butter, melted

1 egg

1. Preheat oven to 350°F. Grease 8×4-inch loaf pan. Measure 2 tablespoons wheat germ; set aside.

2. Attach flat beater to stand mixer. Combine remaining wheat germ, flours, brown sugar, baking soda, baking powder and salt in large bowl. Add raisins; stir until coated.

3. Whisk buttermilk, butter and egg in small bowl until blended. Add to flour mixture; mix on low speed just until blended. Pour into prepared pan; sprinkle with reserved 2 tablespoons wheat germ.

4. Bake 40 to 50 minutes or until toothpick inserted into center comes out clean. Cool in pan on wire rack 10 minutes. Remove to wire rack; cool at least 30 minutes.

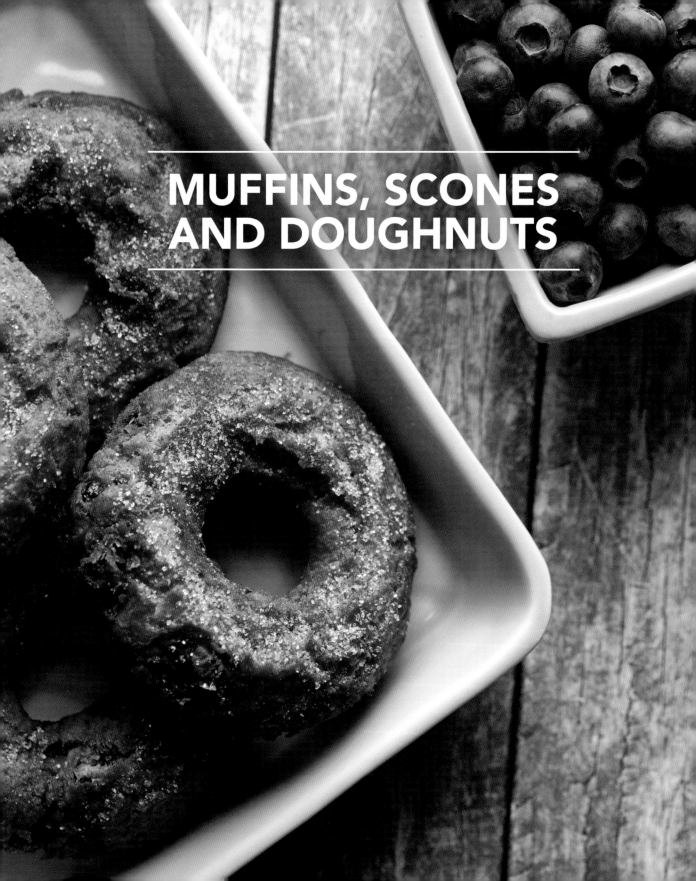

MUFFINS, SCONES AND DOUGHNUTS

BLUEBERRY DOUGHNUTS

MAKES 14 TO 16 DOUGHNUTS

2¾ cups all-purpose flour

¼ cup cornstarch

1 teaspoon salt

1 teaspoon baking powder

½ teaspoon baking soda

1½ teaspoons ground cinnamon, divided

½ teaspoon ground nutmeg

1½ cups sugar, divided

2 eggs

¼ cup (½ stick) butter, melted

¼ cup applesauce

1 teaspoon vanilla

½ cup buttermilk

1 cup drained canned blueberries, patted dry with paper towels

1. Whisk flour, cornstarch, salt, baking powder, baking soda, ½ teaspoon cinnamon and nutmeg in large bowl.

2. Attach flat beater to stand mixer. Beat 1 cup sugar and eggs in mixer bowl on high speed 3 minutes or until pale and thick. Stir in butter, applesauce and vanilla on medium speed. Add flour mixture alternately with buttermilk, mixing on low speed after each addition. Press plastic wrap directly onto surface of dough; refrigerate 1 at least hour.

3. Pour about 2 inches of oil into Dutch oven or large heavy saucepan; clip deep-fry or candy thermometer to side of pot. Heat over medium-high heat to 365°F to 375°F.

4. Meanwhile, generously flour work surface. Add blueberries to dough; knead in gently. Turn out dough onto work surface and dust top with flour. Roll dough about ¼-inch thick; cut out doughnuts with floured doughnut cutter. Gather and reroll scraps. For topping, combine remaining ½ cup sugar and 1 teaspoon cinnamon in large bowl. Line large wire rack with paper towels.

5. Working in batches, add doughnuts to hot oil. Cook 1 minute per side or until golden brown. Do not crowd pan and adjust heat to maintain temperature during frying. Drain doughnuts briefly on prepared wire rack, then sprinkle with cinnamon-sugar topping. Cool on wire racks.

PUMPKIN PECAN MUFFINS

MAKES 12 SERVINGS

8 tablespoons sugar, divided

3 teaspoons ground
   cinnamon, divided

1 cup 100% bran cereal

1 cup milk

1 cup all-purpose flour

1 tablespoon baking powder

½ teaspoon baking soda

½ teaspoon salt

1 cup canned pumpkin puree

1 egg, beaten

1 tablespoon vanilla

1 package (2 ounces) pecan
   chips (½ cup)

1. Preheat oven to 400°F. Grease 12 standard (2½-inch) muffin cups or line with paper baking cups. Combine 2 tablespoons sugar and 1 teaspoon cinnamon in small bowl for topping; set aside.

2. Attach flat beater to stand mixer. Combine cereal and milk in mixer bowl; set aside 5 minutes to soften. Meanwhile, combine flour, remaining 6 tablespoons sugar, remaining cinnamon, baking powder, baking soda and salt in large bowl; mix well.

3. Add pumpkin, egg and vanilla to cereal mixture; mix on low speed until well blended. Add flour mixture; mix just until blended. *Do not overmix.* Spoon batter evenly into prepared muffin cups; sprinkle with pecan chips and cinnamon-sugar topping.

4. Bake 20 to 25 minutes or until toothpick inserted into centers comes out clean. Cool in pan on wire rack 3 minutes. Remove to wire rack. Serve warm.

CARAMELIZED ONION–BACON MUFFINS

MAKES 12 SERVINGS

6 **slices bacon, chopped**
2 **cups chopped onions**
3 **teaspoons sugar, divided**
¼ **teaspoon dried thyme**
1½ **cups all-purpose flour**
¾ **cup grated Parmesan cheese**
2 **teaspoons baking powder**
½ **teaspoon salt**
¾ **cup lager or other light-colored beer**
2 **eggs**
¼ **cup extra virgin olive oil**

1. Preheat oven to 375°F. Grease 12 standard (2½-inch) muffin cups.

2. Cook bacon in large skillet over medium heat until crisp, stirring occasionally. Drain on paper towel-lined plate. Add onions, 1 teaspoon sugar and thyme to skillet; cook 12 minutes or until onions are golden brown, stirring occasionally. Cool 5 minutes; stir in bacon.

3. Attach flat beater to stand mixer. Combine flour, cheese, baking powder, salt and remaining 2 teaspoons sugar in mixer bowl. Whisk lager, eggs and oil in medium bowl. Add to flour mixture; mix on low speed just until blended. Gently stir in onion mixture. Spoon batter evenly into prepared muffin cups.

4. Bake 15 minutes or until toothpick inserted into centers comes out clean. Cool in pan 5 minutes; remove to wire rack. Serve warm.

LEMON POPPY SEED MUFFINS

MAKES 18 MUFFINS

2 cups all-purpose flour

1¼ cups granulated sugar

¼ cup poppy seeds

2 tablespoons plus
2 teaspoons grated lemon
peel, divided

2 teaspoons baking powder

½ teaspoon baking soda

½ teaspoon ground
cardamom

¼ teaspoon salt

2 eggs

½ cup (1 stick) butter, melted

½ cup milk

½ cup plus 2 tablespoons
lemon juice, divided

1 cup powdered sugar

1. Preheat oven to 400°F. Grease 18 standard (2½-inch) muffin cups or line with paper baking cups.

2. Attach flat beater to stand mixer. Combine flour, granulated sugar, poppy seeds, 2 tablespoons lemon peel, baking powder, baking soda, cardamom and salt in large bowl.

3. Whisk eggs in medium bowl. Add butter, milk and ½ cup lemon juice; mix well. Add to flour mixture; mix on low speed just until blended. Spoon batter evenly into prepared muffin cups.

4. Bake 15 to 20 minutes or until toothpick inserted into centers comes out clean. Cool in pans on wire racks 10 minutes.

5. Meanwhile for glaze, combine powdered sugar and remaining 2 teaspoons lemon peel in small bowl; whisk in enough remaining lemon juice to make pourable glaze. Drizzle over muffins. Let stand until glaze sets. Serve warm or at room temperature.

SUGAR AND SPICE DOUGHNUTS

MAKES 14 TO 16 DOUGHNUTS

2¾ cups all-purpose flour

¼ cup cornstarch

1 teaspoon salt

1 teaspoon baking powder

½ teaspoon baking soda

½ teaspoon ground cinnamon

½ teaspoon ground nutmeg

1 cup sugar

2 eggs

¼ cup (½ stick) butter, melted

¼ cup applesauce

1 teaspoon vanilla

½ cup buttermilk

Vegetable oil for frying

TOPPING

1 cup sugar

1 teaspoon ground cinnamon

1. Whisk flour, cornstarch, salt, baking powder, baking soda, ½ teaspoon cinnamon and nutmeg in large bowl.

2. Attach flat beater to stand mixer. Beat 1 cup sugar and eggs in mixer bowl on high speed 3 minutes or until pale and thick. Stir in butter, applesauce and vanilla on medium speed. Add flour mixture alternately with buttermilk, mixing on low speed after each addition. Press plastic wrap directly onto surface of dough; refrigerate 1 at least hour.

3. Pour about 2 inches of oil into Dutch oven or large heavy saucepan; clip deep-fry or candy thermometer to side of pot. Heat over medium-high heat to 365°F to 375°F. Line large wire rack with paper towels.

4. Meanwhile, generously flour work surface. Turn out dough onto work surface and dust top with flour. Roll dough about ¼-inch thick; cut out doughnuts with floured doughnut cutter. Gather and reroll scraps. For topping, combine 1 cup sugar and 1 teaspoon cinnamon in large bowl.

5. Working in batches, add doughnuts to hot oil. Cook 1 minute per side or until golden brown. Do not crowd pan and adjust heat to maintain temperature during frying. Drain briefly on prepared wire rack, then toss in topping to coat both sides. Cool on wire racks.

ENGLISH–STYLE SCONES

MAKES 6 SCONES

3 **eggs, divided**

½ **cup heavy cream**

1½ **teaspoons vanilla**

2 **cups all-purpose flour**

2 **teaspoons baking powder**

¼ **teaspoon salt**

¼ **cup (½ stick) cold butter, cut into small pieces**

¼ **cup finely chopped pitted dates**

¼ **cup golden raisins or currants**

1 **teaspoon water**

6 **tablespoons orange marmalade fruit spread**

6 **tablespoons crème fraîche**

1. Preheat oven to 375°F. Line large baking sheet with parchment paper.

2. Whisk 2 eggs, cream and vanilla in medium bowl. Attach flat beater to stand mixer. Combine flour, baking powder and salt in mixer bowl. Add butter; mix on low speed until mixture resembles coarse crumbs. Stir in dates and raisins. Add cream mixture; mix on low speed just until dry ingredients are moistened.

3. Turn out dough onto lightly floured surface; knead four times with floured hands. Place dough on prepared baking sheet; pat into 8-inch circle. Score dough into six wedges with sharp wet knife, cutting three-fourths of the way through. Beat remaining egg and water in small bowl; brush lightly over dough.

4. Bake 18 to 20 minutes or until golden brown. Cool 5 minutes on wire rack. Cut into wedges; serve warm with marmalade and crème fraîche.

RASPBERRY CORN MUFFINS

MAKES 12 MUFFINS

- 1 **cup all-purpose flour**
- ¾ **cup yellow cornmeal**
- 2 **teaspoons baking powder**
- ½ **teaspoon baking soda**
- ¼ **teaspoon salt**
- 1 **cup sour cream**
- ⅓ **cup thawed frozen unsweetened apple juice concentrate**
- 1 **egg**
- 1½ **cups fresh or frozen raspberries**

1. Preheat oven to 350°F. Grease 12 standard (2½-inch) muffin cups.

2. Attach flat beater to stand mixer. Combine flour, cornmeal, baking powder, baking soda and salt in mixer bowl. Whisk sour cream, apple juice concentrate and egg in small bowl. Add to flour mixture; mix on low speed just until moistened. Gently stir in raspberries. Spoon batter into prepared muffin cups.

3. Bake 18 to 20 minutes or until golden brown. Cool in pan on wire rack 5 minutes. Remove from pan; cool slightly.

SOUR CREAM DOUGHNUTS

MAKES 14 TO 16 DOUGHNUTS

2¾ cups all-purpose flour

¼ cup cornstarch

1 teaspoon salt

1 teaspoon baking powder

½ teaspoon baking soda

½ teaspoon ground nutmeg

1 cup granulated sugar

¼ cup (½ stick) butter, softened

2 eggs

1 cup sour cream

1 teaspoon vanilla

Vegetable oil for frying

CHOCOLATE GLAZE

½ cup plus 2 tablespoons heavy cream or half-and-half, divided

1 cup semisweet or dark chocolate chips

1 tablespoon butter

½ cup powdered sugar

Sprinkles or decors (optional)

1. Whisk flour, cornstarch, salt, baking powder, baking soda and nutmeg in large bowl.

2. Attach flat beater to stand mixer. Beat granulated sugar and ¼ cup butter in mixer bowl on medium speed until crumbly and blended. Add eggs, one at a time, beating until well blended after each addition. Beat in sour cream and vanilla. Add flour mixture; beat on low speed just until blended. Press plastic wrap directly onto surface of dough; refrigerate at least 1 hour.

3. Pour about 2 inches of oil into Dutch oven or large heavy saucepan; clip deep-fry or candy thermometer to side of pot. Heat over medium-high heat to 365°F to 375°F. Line large wire rack with paper towels.

4. Meanwhile, generously flour work surface. Turn out dough onto work surface and dust top with flour. Roll dough about ¼-inch thick; cut out doughnuts with floured doughnut cutter. Gather and reroll scraps.

5. Working in batches, add doughnuts to hot oil. Cook 1 minute per side or until golden brown. Do not crowd pan and adjust heat to maintain temperature during frying. Drain on prepared wire rack.

6. For glaze, heat ½ cup cream in small saucepan over low heat until bubbles form around edge of pan. Stir in chocolate chips and 1 tablespoon butter until melted and smooth. Whisk in powdered sugar and enough remaining cream to make medium thick pourable glaze. Cook about 1 minute or until smooth and warm. Dip tops of doughnuts in glaze; place on wire rack. Decorate as desired; let stand until set.

STREUSEL RASPBERRY MUFFINS

MAKES 12 MUFFINS

- ¼ cup chopped pecans
- ¼ cup packed brown sugar
- 1¾ cups all-purpose flour, divided
- ½ cup (1 stick) plus 2 tablespoons butter, melted and cooled, divided
- ½ cup granulated sugar
- 2 teaspoons baking powder
- ½ cup milk
- 1 egg, beaten
- 1 cup fresh frozen raspberries

1. Preheat oven to 375°F. Grease 12 standard (2½-inch) muffin cups or line with paper baking cups. Combine pecans, brown sugar and ¼ cup all-purpose flour. Stir in 2 tablespoons melted butter until mixture resembles moist crumbs.

2. Attach flat beater to stand mixer. Combine remaining 1½ cups flour, granulated sugar and baking powder in mixer bowl. Whisk milk, remaining ½ cup butter and egg in small bowl. Add to flour mixture; mix on low speed just until moistened.

3. Spoon half of batter into muffin cups. Divide raspberries among cups; top with remaining batter. Sprinkle with topping. Bake 25 to 30 minutes or until toothpick inserted into centers comes out clean. Cool in pan on wire rack 5 minutes; remove to rack to cool.

ORANGE–CURRANT SCONES

MAKES 8 SCONES

1½ cups all-purpose flour

¼ cup plus 1 teaspoon sugar, divided

1 teaspoon baking powder

¼ teaspoon salt

¼ teaspoon baking soda

⅓ cup currants

1 tablespoon grated orange peel

6 tablespoons (¾ stick) cold butter, cut into small pieces

½ cup buttermilk, yogurt or sour cream

1. Preheat oven to 425°F. Grease baking sheet or line with parchment paper.

2. Attach flat beater to stand mixer. Combine flour, ¼ cup sugar, baking powder, salt and baking soda in mixer bowl. Stir in currants and orange peel. Add butter; mix on low speed until mixture resembles coarse crumbs. Add buttermilk; stir until mixture forms soft sticky dough that clings together.

3. Shape dough into a ball; pat into 8-inch round on prepared baking sheet. Cut into eight wedges with floured knife. Sprinkle with remaining 1 teaspoon sugar.

4. Bake 18 to 20 minutes or until lightly browned. Remove to wire rack to cool slightly. Serve warm.

LEMON–FILLED DOUGHNUTS

MAKES 12 DOUGHNUTS

Lemon Curd (page 126) or
  prepared lemon curd

½ cup water

½ cup milk

1 tablespoon active dry yeast

½ cup plus 1 teaspoon
  granulated sugar, divided

½ cup (1 stick) butter,
  softened

3 eggs

½ teaspoon vanilla

3½ cups all-purpose flour,
  divided

¾ teaspoon salt

Powdered sugar

1. Prepare Lemon Curd. Heat water and milk in small saucepan to about 115°F. Transfer to small bowl; stir in yeast and 1 teaspoon sugar. Let stand 5 minutes or until mixture is bubbly.

2. Attach flat beater to stand mixer. Beat butter and remaining ½ cup sugar in mixer bowl on medium speed until light and fluffy. Add eggs, one at a time, beating well after each addition. Beat in vanilla. Reduce speed to low; beat in yeast mixture, 1½ cups flour and salt. Beat on medium speed 2 minutes.

3. Replace flat beater with dough hook. Add remaining 2 cups flour. Beat on low speed until most of flour is incorporated. Beat on medium speed 3 minutes (dough will be sticky). Cover and let rise in warm place about 1½ hours or until doubled. Stir down dough. Cover and refrigerate 2 hours or overnight.

4. Pour about 2 inches of oil into Dutch oven or large heavy saucepan; clip deep-fry or candy thermometer to side of pot. Heat over medium-high heat to 365°F. Line large wire rack with paper towels.

5. Meanwhile, turn out dough onto lightly floured surface. Roll ¼ inch thick. Cut out circles with 2-inch biscuit cutter. Working in batches, add dough to hot oil. Cook 1½ minutes per side or until golden brown. Do not crowd pan and adjust heat to maintain temperature. Drain on prepared wire rack.

6. Fit pastry bag with small round tip. Fill bag with lemon curd. Insert thin knife into side of each doughnut and twist to make room for filling. Fill doughnuts; sprinkle with powdered sugar.

PEANUT BUTTER BRAN MUFFINS

MAKES 12 MUFFINS

½ **cup peanut butter**

2 **tablespoons butter**

¼ **cup packed brown sugar**

1 **egg**

1 **cup whole bran cereal**

1 **cup milk**

¾ **cup all-purpose flour**

1 **tablespoon baking powder**

½ **teaspoon salt**

½ **cup raisins**

1. Preheat oven to 400°F. Grease 12 standard (2½-inch) muffin cups or line with paper baking cups.

2. Attach flat beater to stand mixer. Combine peanut butter, butter, brown sugar and egg in mixer bowl; beat on medium speed until smooth. Add cereal and milk; mix on low speed just until blended.

3. Add flour, baking powder and salt; mix on low speed just until flour is moistened. Batter should be lumpy. Add raisins; mix just until blended. Spoon batter evenly into prepared muffin cups.

4. Bake about 20 minutes or until toothpick inserted into centers comes out clean. Cool in pan on wire rack 5 minutes. Remove to wire rack; serve warm.

CHERRY–LEMON POPPY SEED MUFFINS

MAKES 12 MUFFINS

2 cups all-purpose flour

1 cup sugar

1 tablespoon baking powder

1 teaspoon salt

¾ cup buttermilk

¼ cup vegetable oil

¼ cup (½ stick) butter, melted

2 eggs

Grated peel of 1 lemon

1 tablespoon fresh lemon juice

1 teaspoon vanilla

½ cup dried sweet cherries, chopped

½ cup chopped pecans

2 tablespoons poppy seeds

1. Preheat oven to 350°F. Grease 12 standard (2½-inch) muffin cups or line with paper baking cups.

2. Attach flat beater to stand mixer. Combine flour, sugar, baking powder and salt in mixer bowl.

3. Whisk buttermilk, oil, butter, eggs, lemon peel, lemon juice and vanilla in medium bowl. Add to flour mixture; mix on low speed just until blended. Stir in cherries, pecans and poppy seeds. Spoon batter evenly into prepared muffin cups.

4. Bake about 20 minutes or until golden brown and toothpick inserted into centers comes out clean. Cool in pan on wire rack 5 minutes. Remove to wire rack; serve warm.

COCONUT SCONES WITH ORANGE BUTTER

MAKES 8 SCONES

1¾ cups all-purpose flour

½ teaspoon salt

1 tablespoon baking powder

2 tablespoons sugar

5 tablespoons cold butter, cut into small pieces

1 egg

1 cup heavy cream, divided

2 tablespoons milk

2 teaspoons grated orange peel

½ cup plus ⅓ cup sweetened flaked coconut, divided

Orange Butter (recipe follows)

1. Preheat oven to 400°F. Line baking sheet with parchment paper.

2. Attach flat beater to stand mixer. Combine flour, salt, baking powder and sugar in mixer bowl. Add butter; mix on low speed until mixture resembles coarse crumbs.

3. Whisk egg, ¾ cup cream, milk, orange peel and ½ cup coconut in small bowl. Add to flour mixture; mix on low speed just until dough forms.

4. Transfer dough to lightly floured surface. Pat into 8-inch circle, about ¾-inch thick. Cut into 8 wedges. Brush tops of scones with remaining ¼ cup cream; sprinkle with remaining ⅓ cup coconut.

5. Place scones 2 inches apart on prepared baking sheet. Bake 12 to 15 minutes or until scones are golden brown and coconut is toasted. Remove to wire rack; cool at least 15 minutes. Prepare Orange Butter; serve with warm scones.

ORANGE BUTTER

MAKES ABOUT ½ CUP

½ cup (1 stick) butter, softened

2 tablespoons fresh orange juice

1 tablespoon grated orange peel

2 teaspoons sugar

Attach flat beater to stand mixer. Beat butter, orange juice, orange peel and sugar in mixer bowl on low speed until creamy and well blended.

COFFEECAKES AND BRUNCH BREADS

CINNAMINI MONKEY BREAD

MAKES ABOUT 16 SERVINGS

3 cups all-purpose flour

1 package (¼ ounce) rapid-rise active dry yeast

1 teaspoon salt

1 cup warm water (120°F)

2 tablespoons butter, melted

5 tablespoons butter, very soft, divided

½ cup packed brown sugar

2 teaspoons ground cinnamon

¼ teaspoon coarse salt

1 cup powdered sugar

2 ounces cream cheese, softened

3 tablespoons milk

1. Attach dough hook to stand mixer. Combine flour, yeast and 1 teaspoon salt in mixer bowl. Stir in water and melted butter with wooden spoon to form rough dough. Knead on low speed 5 to 7 minutes or until dough is smooth and elastic.

2. Shape dough into a ball. Place in large lightly greased bowl; turn once to grease surface. Cover and let rise in warm place about 1 hour or until doubled in size.

3. Grease 12-cup (10-inch) bundt pan with 1 tablespoon soft butter. Combine brown sugar, cinnamon and coarse salt in shallow bowl. Turn out dough onto lightly floured surface. Roll dough into 24×16-inch rectangle; cut lengthwise into four strips.

4. Spread 1 tablespoon softened butter over each dough strip; sprinkle evenly with cinnamon-sugar, pressing gently to adhere. Starting with long side, roll up dough jelly-roll style; pinch seam to seal. Cut crosswise into 1-inch slices; place slices in prepared pan with cut sides of slices against side of pan. Cover and let rise in warm place 30 minutes or until dough is puffy.

5. Preheat oven to 350°F. Bake 20 to 25 minutes or until bread is firm and lightly browned. Loosen edges of bread with knife; immediately invert onto serving plate. Cool slightly.

6. For glaze, attach wire whip to stand mixer. Combine powdered sugar, cream cheese and milk in mixer bowl; whip on medium speed until smooth. Drizzle glaze over bread. Serve warm.

Tip: Serve remaining glaze with bread for dipping.

CHERRY, ALMOND AND CHOCOLATE TWIST

MAKES 1 RING

1 cup dried sweet or sour cherries

½ cup granulated sugar, divided

¼ cup warm water (105° to 115°F)

1 package (¼ ounce) active dry yeast

½ cup plus 1 tablespoon milk, divided

3 tablespoons butter, cut into small pieces

2 eggs, divided

1 tablespoon grated lemon peel

½ teaspoon salt

½ teaspoon almond extract

2½ to 2¾ cups all-purpose flour

½ cup canned almond filling (about 12 ounces)

¾ cup semisweet chocolate chips

Almond Glaze (recipe follows)

1. Combine 1 cup water, cherries and ¼ cup sugar in small saucepan; bring to a boil over high heat, stirring constantly. Remove from heat; cover and set aside.

2. Attach flat beater to stand mixer. Pour ¼ cup warm water into mixer bowl. Sprinkle yeast over water; stir to dissolve yeast. Let stand 5 minutes.

3. Meanwhile, heat ½ cup milk and butter in medium saucepan over medium heat until milk is warm (115°F); butter does not need to melt completely. Remove from heat; stir occasionally until milk is warm to the touch.

4. Add milk mixture to yeast mixture. Stir in remaining ¼ cup granulated sugar, 1 egg, lemon peel, salt and almond extract until well blended. Replace flat beater with dough hook. Add 2¼ cups flour; beat until dough forms a sticky ball. Add enough remaining flour to form soft dough. Knead on medium-low speed about 5 minutes or until smooth and elastic, adding additional flour to prevent sticking if necessary. Shape dough into a ball. Place in large lightly greased bowl; turn once to grease surface. Cover and let rise in warm place about 1 hours or until doubled in size.

5. Preheat oven to 350°F. Line large baking sheet with parchment paper. Punch down dough. Turn out dough onto lightly floured surface; knead 10 to 12 times or until dough is smooth. Shape dough into 10-inch log. Flatten slightly. Roll out dough into 18×8-inch rectangle with lightly floured rolling pin. Transfer dough to prepared baking sheet

6. Drain cherries. Spread almond filling evenly over dough; sprinkle with cherries and chocolate chips. Cut dough at 1½-inch intervals to within ¾ inch of center with sharp knife. Gently lift each section and turn on its side, overlapping slices. Whisk remaining egg and 1 tablespoon milk in small bowl until well blended; brush over dough.

7. Bake 30 minutes or until golden brown. Cool on baking sheet 5 minutes. Remove to wire rack to cool.

8. Prepare Almond Glaze; drizzle over coffeecake. Let stand until set.

Almond Glaze: Combine ½ cup powdered sugar, 2 teaspoons milk and ¼ teaspoon almond extract in small bowl until smooth. Add additional milk, 1 teaspoon at a time, until glaze is of desired consistency.

TRIPLE CHOCOLATE STICKY BUNS

MAKES 12 ROLLS

DOUGH

2¾ cups bread flour

⅓ cup unsweetened cocoa powder

¼ cup granulated sugar

1 package (¼ ounce) rapid-rise active dry yeast

1 teaspoon salt

½ cup sour cream

1 egg

¼ cup warm water (130°F)

3 tablespoons butter, softened

TOPPING

⅓ cup packed brown sugar

¼ cup (½ stick) butter

2 tablespoons light corn syrup

1 tablespoon unsweetened cocoa powder

FILLING

¼ cup packed brown sugar

½ teaspoon ground cinnamon

3 tablespoons butter, melted

½ to ¾ cup coarsely chopped walnuts, toasted*

½ cup semisweet chocolate chips

To toast walnuts, spread in single layer on baking sheet. Bake in preheated 350°F oven 8 to 10 minutes or until golden brown, stirring frequently.

1. Attach flat beater to stand mixer. Combine flour, cocoa, ¼ cup granulated sugar, yeast and salt in mixer bowl. Whisk sour cream and egg in small bowl until well blended. Add water, butter and sour cream mixture to flour mixture; beat on medium speed 3 minutes.

2. Replace flat beater with dough hook; knead on medium-low speed about 6 minutes. Place dough in large lightly greased bowl; turn once to grease surface. Cover and let rise in warm place about 40 minutes. (Dough will not double in size.)

3. Grease 9-inch round cake pan. For topping, combine ⅓ cup brown sugar, ¼ cup butter, corn syrup and 1 tablespoon cocoa in small saucepan; heat over medium heat until brown sugar dissolves and mixture bubbles around edge, stirring frequently. Pour into prepared pan. For filling, combine ¼ cup brown sugar and cinnamon in small bowl.

4. Turn out dough onto lightly floured surface. Roll into 12×8-inch rectangle. Brush with melted butter and sprinkle with brown sugar mixture. Sprinkle with walnuts and chocolate chips; gently press into dough. Starting with long side, roll up tightly and pinch seam to seal. Cut crosswise into 12 slices; arrange slices cut sides up over topping in pan. Cover and let rise in warm place about 35 minutes or until doubled in size.

5. Preheat oven to 375°F. Bake about 25 minutes or just until buns in center of pan are firm to the touch. Immediately invert onto serving plate. Serve warm or at room temperature.

ORANGE POPPY SEED SWEET ROLLS

MAKES 12 ROLLS

DOUGH

- 3 **cups bread flour**
- ¼ **cup granulated sugar**
- 1 **tablespoon poppy seeds**
- 2 **teaspoons active dry yeast**
- 1 **teaspoon salt**
- ¾ **cup orange juice, at room temperature***
- 5 **tablespoons butter, melted, divided**
- 1 **egg**

ICING

- 1 **cup powdered sugar**
- 4 **teaspoons orange juice**
- ¾ **to 1 teaspoon grated orange peel**

To bring orange juice to room temperature, place in 2-cup microwavable glass measure and heat on HIGH 10 to 15 seconds.

1. Attach flat beater to stand mixer. Combine flour, granulated sugar, poppy seeds, yeast and salt in mixer bowl. Whisk ¾ cup orange juice, 4 tablespoons butter and egg in small bowl. Add to flour mixture; knead on low speed 5 to 7 minutes or until dough is smooth and elastic.

2. Shape dough into a ball. Place in large lightly greased bowl; turn once to grease surface. Cover and let rise in warm place 1 hour or until doubled.

3. Turn out dough onto lightly floured surface. Divide dough into 12 equal pieces. Shape each piece into 10-inch rope; coil each rope and tuck end under coil. Place in prepared pan. Brush remaining 1 tablespoon butter over rolls. Cover and let rise in warm place 1 to 1½ hours or until doubled.

4. Preheat oven to 350°F. Bake 20 minutes or until golden brown. Remove to wire rack to cool.

5. For icing, combine powdered sugar, 4 teaspoons orange juice and orange peel in medium bowl until smooth; spread over rolls.

APPLE RING COFFEECAKE

MAKES 12 SERVINGS

- 3 **cups all-purpose flour**
- 1 **teaspoon baking soda**
- 1 **teaspoon salt**
- 1 **teaspoon ground cinnamon**
- 1 **cup chopped walnuts**
- 1½ **cups granulated sugar**
- 1 **cup vegetable oil**
- 2 **eggs**
- 2 **teaspoons vanilla**
- 2 **medium tart apples, peeled and chopped**
- **Powdered sugar (optional)**

1. Preheat oven to 325°F. Grease 10-inch tube pan.

2. Attach flat beater to stand mixer. Sift flour, baking soda, salt and cinnamon into mixer bowl. Stir in walnuts; set aside.

3. Combine granulated sugar, oil, eggs and vanilla in medium bowl. Add to flour mixture; mix on low speed just until moistened. Stir in apples. Spoon batter into prepared pan, spreading evenly.

4. Bake 1 hour or until toothpick inserted near center comes out clean. Cool in pan on wire rack 10 minutes. Loosen edges with metal spatula, if necessary. Remove from pan; cool completely on wire rack. Sprinkle with powdered sugar just before serving, if desired.

CHERRY BUTTERMILK LOOPS

MAKES 16 ROLLS

⅓ cup chopped dried cherries

½ cup water

½ cup warm buttermilk (110° to 115°F)

1 egg

3 tablespoons butter, softened

3 cups bread flour

¼ cup granulated sugar

2 teaspoons active dry yeast

1 teaspoon salt

¼ cup cherry preserves, large cherry pieces chopped

1⅓ cups powdered sugar

3 tablespoons cold buttermilk

¼ cup sliced almonds, toasted*

*To toast almonds, spread in single layer on baking sheet. Bake in preheated 350°F oven 8 to 10 minutes or until golden brown, stirring frequently.

1. Place cherries and water in small microwavable bowl; cover. Microwave on HIGH 30 seconds; let stand 5 minutes. Drain cherries; reserve ¼ cup soaking liquid in medium bowl. Whisk in warm buttermilk, egg and butter until well blended.

2. Attach flat beater to stand mixer. Combine 2 cups flour, granulated sugar, yeast and salt in mixer bowl; mix on low speed 10 seconds. Add buttermilk mixture; mix on medium-low speed until rough dough forms. Replace flat beater with dough hook; knead on low speed 5 to 7 minutes, adding additional 1 cup flour as needed until dough is smooth and elastic. Shape dough into a ball. Place in large lightly greased bowl; turn once to grease surface. Cover and let rise in warm place about 1 hour or until doubled.

3. Lightly grease two baking sheets. Turn out dough onto lightly floured surface. Divide dough into 16 pieces. Gently roll and stretch each piece into 7-inch-long rope. Shape each rope into loop with ends crossed; place on prepared baking sheets. Cover and let rise in warm place about 45 minutes or until doubled in size.

4. Preheat oven to 375°F. Bake 12 to 15 minutes or until golden brown. Meanwhile, heat preserves in small saucepan over low heat until slightly warmed and softened but not melted. Remove rolls from oven. Immediately brush entire surfaces generously with warm preserves. Remove to wire racks to cool.

5. Combine powdered sugar and cold buttermilk in small bowl, stirring until smooth. Place waxed paper under wire racks. Drizzle icing over rolls. Sprinkle with almonds.

PECAN–CINNAMON STICKY BUNS

MAKES 12 BUNS

3 to 3½ cups all-purpose flour

1 package (¼ ounce) rapid-rise active dry yeast

1 teaspoon salt

1 cup milk

¾ cup plus 2 tablespoons honey, divided

1 egg, beaten

5 tablespoons butter, melted, divided

¾ cup chopped pecans

¼ cup packed brown sugar

2 teaspoons ground cinnamon

1. Attach flat beater to stand mixer. Combine 3 cups flour, yeast and salt in large bowl. Place milk and 2 tablespoons honey in small saucepan; heat until very warm (120°F), stirring to dissolve honey. Add to flour mixture; mix on low speed until blended. Beat in egg and 3 tablespoons melted butter until dough forms.

2. Replace flat beater with dough hook. Knead on low speed 5 to 7 minutes or until dough is smooth and elastic, adding additional flour to prevent sticking. Shape dough into a ball. Place in large lightly greased bowl; turn once to grease surface. Cover and let rise in warm place 30 to 40 minutes or until doubled in size.

3. Spread remaining ¾ cup honey evenly in bottom of 9-inch baking pan; sprinkle with pecans.

4. Punch down dough; turn out onto floured surface. Pat or roll dough into 15×9-inch rectangle. Brush dough with remaining 2 tablespoons butter. Mix brown sugar and cinnamon in small bowl; sprinkle over butter. Roll up dough from long side into log; pinch edges to seal. Cut into 12 slices about 1¼ inches thick. Arrange in prepared pan; cover and let rise 25 minutes.

5. Preheat oven to 350°F. Bake 30 minutes or until golden. Cool slightly; invert onto plate.

MAPLE BACON BUBBLE BREAD

MAKES 12 SERVINGS

3 cups all-purpose flour

1 package (¼ ounce) rapid-rise active dry yeast

1½ teaspoons salt

1 cup warm water (120°F)

2 tablespoons olive oil

10 slices bacon, cooked and coarsely chopped (about 12 ounces)

¼ cup packed brown sugar

¼ teaspoon black pepper

3 tablespoons butter

3 tablespoons maple syrup

1. Attach dough hook to stand mixer. Combine flour, yeast and salt in mixer bowl. Stir in water and 2 tablespoons oil with wooden spoon to form rough dough. Knead on low speed 5 to 7 minutes or until dough is smooth and elastic.

2. Shape dough into a ball. Place in large lightly greased bowl; turn once to grease surface. Cover and let rise in warm place 30 to 45 minutes or until doubled in size.

3. Combine bacon, brown sugar and pepper in medium bowl. Combine butter and maple syrup in medium microwavable bowl; microwave on HIGH 30 seconds; stir. Microwave 20 seconds or until butter is melted.

4. Grease 12-cup (10-inch) bundt pan.

5. Roll 1-inch pieces of dough into balls. Dip balls in butter mixture; roll in bacon mixture to coat. Layer in prepared pan. Reheat any remaining butter mixture, if necessary; drizzle over top of dough. Cover and let rise in warm place about 45 minutes or until doubled in size.

6. Preheat oven to 350°F. Bake 30 to 35 minutes or until golden brown. Cool in pan on wire rack 5 minutes. Loosen edges of bread with knife; invert onto serving plate. Serve warm.

RASPBERRY BREAKFAST RING

MAKES 16 SERVINGS

½ **cup warm milk (105° to 115°F)**

⅓ **cup warm water (105° to 115°F)**

1 **package (¼ ounce) active dry yeast**

3 **to 3¼ cups all-purpose flour, divided**

1 **egg**

3 **tablespoons butter, melted**

3 **tablespoons granulated sugar**

1 **teaspoon salt**

¼ **cup red raspberry fruit spread**

1 **teaspoon grated orange peel**

Powdered sugar

Sliced almonds (optional)

1. Attach flat beater to stand mixer. Combine milk and water in small saucepan. Heat over medium heat to 115°F. Pour milk mixture into mixer bowl. Stir in yeast until dissolved. Let stand 5 minutes.

2. Add 2¾ cups flour, egg, butter, granulated sugar and salt; beat on medium-low speed until soft dough forms. Replace flat beater with dough hook. Knead on low speed about 5 to 7 minutes or until dough is smooth and elastic, adding remaining flour if needed to prevent sticking. Place dough in large lightly greased bowl; turn once to grease surface. Cover and let rise in warm place about 1 hour or until doubled in size.

3. Punch dough down. Cover and let rest in warm place 10 minutes. Line large baking sheet with parchment paper. Combine fruit spread and orange peel in small bowl; mix well.

4. Roll out dough into 16×9-inch rectangle on lightly floured surface. Spread raspberry mixture evenly over dough. Starting with long side, tightly roll up dough; pinch seam to seal. Shape dough into ring on prepared baking sheet, keeping seam side down and pinching ends to seal.

5. Use serrated knife to cut slices three fourths of the way through dough at 1-inch intervals. Slightly twist each cut section of dough, forming many rings. Cover loosely with plastic wrap and let rise in warm place 30 to 45 minutes or until doubled in size.

6. Preheat oven to 350°F. Bake about 25 minutes or until lightly browned. Remove to wire rack; cool completely. Dust with powdered sugar and garnish with almonds.

SWEET AND SAVORY SNACKS

PULL-APART GARLIC CHEESE BREAD

MAKES 12 SERVINGS

- 3 cups all-purpose flour
- 1 package (¼ ounce) rapid-rise active dry yeast
- 1 teaspoon salt
- 1 cup warm water (120°F)
- 2 tablespoons olive oil
- 6 cloves garlic, minced, divided
- ¼ cup (½ stick) butter
- ¼ teaspoon paprika
- 1 cup grated Parmesan cheese
- 1 cup (4 ounces) shredded mozzarella cheese
- ½ cup pizza sauce

1. Attach dough hook to stand mixer. Combine flour, yeast and salt in mixer bowl. Stir in water and oil with wooden spoon to form rough dough; stir in half of garlic. Knead with dough hook on low speed 5 to 7 minutes or until dough is smooth and elastic.

2. Shape dough into a ball. Place in large lightly greased bowl; turn once to grease surface. Cover and let rise in warm place about to 1 hour or until doubled in size.

3. Melt butter in small skillet over medium-low heat. Add remaining garlic; cook and stir 1 minute. Stir in paprika; remove from heat. Brush 9-inch springform pan with some of butter mixture. Place 6-ounce ramekin in center of pan. Line baking sheet with foil. Place Parmesan in shallow bowl.

4. Turn out dough onto lightly floured surface; pat into 9-inch square. Cut into 1-inch squares; roll into balls. Dip half of balls in melted butter mixture; roll in Parmesan to coat. Place around ramekin in prepared pan; sprinkle with ½ cup mozzarella. Repeat layers. Cover and let rise in warm place 1 hour or until dough has risen to top of pan.

5. Preheat oven to 350°F. Pour pizza sauce into ramekin. Place springform pan on prepared baking sheet. Bake 20 to 25 minutes or until bread is firm and golden brown. Loosen edges of bread with knife; carefully remove side of pan. Serve warm with pizza sauce for dipping.

HONEY BUTTER PULL–APART BREAD

MAKES 8 SERVINGS

3 cups all-purpose flour

1 package (¼ ounce) rapid-
   rise active dry yeast

1 teaspoon salt

1 cup warm water (120°F)

2 tablespoons butter, melted

¼ cup (½ stick) butter,
   softened

¼ cup honey

1. Attach dough hook to stand mixer. Combine flour, yeast and salt in mixer bowl. Stir in water and melted butter with wooden spoon to form rough dough. Knead on low speed 5 to 7 minutes or until dough is smooth and elastic.

2. Shape dough into a ball. Place in large lightly greased bowl; turn once to grease surface. Cover and let rise in warm place 1 hour or until doubled in size.

3. Grease 8×4-inch loaf pan. Combine softened butter and honey in small bowl. Turn out dough onto lightly floured surface. Roll into 18×10-inch rectangle; cut in half crosswise to make two 9×10-inch rectangles. Spread some of honey butter over one half of dough; top with remaining half. Cut dough in half crosswise to make two 9×5-inch rectangles. Spread some of honey butter over one half; top with remaining half. Cut dough in half lengthwise, then cut crosswise into 1-inch strips. Place rows of strips vertically in prepared pan. Cover and let rise in warm place 1 hour or until dough is puffy.

4. Preheat oven to 350°F. Brush or dollop remaining honey butter over dough strips. Bake 30 minutes or until bread is firm and golden brown. Immediately remove from pan to wire rack. Serve warm.

MINI PAIN AU CHOCOLATE

MAKES 16 ROLLS

Pie Pastry for Double Crust Pie (page 43)
½ cup sugar
1 cup semisweet chocolate chips

1. Prepare pie pastry.

2. Preheat oven to 400°F. Grease baking sheet or line with parchment paper.

3. Sprinkle ¼ cup sugar on cutting board or work surface. Roll out pastry into two 12-inch squares; sprinkle with ¼ cup sugar.

4. Cut squares in half; cut each half crosswise into 4 pieces to form 8 small (4×2-inch) rectangles. Place heaping teaspoon chocolate chips at one short end of each rectangle; roll up. Place rolls, seam side down, on prepared baking sheet.

5. Bake 12 to 14 minutes or until lightly browned. Remove to wire rack. Serve warm or cool completely.

PRETZEL BITES WITH HONEY MUSTARD

MAKES ABOUT 144 BITES

¾ cup sour cream

¼ cup Dijon mustard

3 tablespoons honey

1⅔ cups warm water (110° to 115°F)

1 package (¼ ounce) rapid-rise active dry yeast

2 teaspoons sugar

½ teaspoon salt

4½ cups all-purpose flour, plus additional for work surface

2 tablespoons butter, softened

12 cups water

½ cup baking soda

Kosher salt or pretzel salt (optional)

1. For honey mustard, stir sour cream, mustard and honey in small bowl until smooth and well blended. Cover and refrigerate until ready to use.

2. Attach flat beater to stand mixer. Combine 1⅔ cups warm water, yeast, sugar and ½ teaspoon salt in mixer bowl. Stir to dissolve yeast. Let stand 5 minutes or until bubbly.

3. Add 4½ cups flour and butter to yeast mixture; mix on low speed until combined. Replace flat beater with dough hook; knead on medium-low speed 5 minutes or until dough is smooth and elastic.

4. Shape dough into a ball. Place in large lightly greased bowl; turn once to grease surface. Cover and let rise in warm place 1 hour or until doubled in size.

5. Preheat oven to 450°F. Grease three baking sheets.

6. Turn out dough onto lightly floured surface. Divide dough into 12 pieces; roll each piece into 12-inch-long rope. Cut each rope into 1-inch pieces.

7. Bring 12 cups water to a boil in large saucepan. Stir in baking soda until dissolved. Working in batches, drop dough pieces into boiling water; boil 30 seconds. Remove with slotted spoon; place on prepared baking sheets. Sprinkle with kosher salt.

8. Bake 12 minutes or until dark golden brown, rotating baking sheets halfway through. Immediately remove from baking sheets. Serve with honey mustard.

BELGIAN LEIGE WAFFLES

MAKES 12 WAFFLES

2 teaspoons active dry yeast

½ teaspoon granulated sugar

½ cup warm milk (120°F)

1½ cups all-purpose flour

2 eggs

2 teaspoons vanilla

1 teaspoon ground cinnamon

½ teaspoon salt

½ cup (1 stick) butter, softened, cut into small pieces

½ cup pearl sugar, turbinado sugar or crushed sugar cubes

1. Attach dough hook to stand mixer. Stir yeast and granulated sugar into warm milk in mixer bowl. Let stand 5 minutes or until bubbly.

2. Add flour, eggs, vanilla and cinnamon and salt to bowl. Knead on low speed until stiff dough forms. Cover bowl with damp towel around dough hook; let rise 30 minutes.

3. Remove towel. With mixer running on low speed, add butter, one piece at a time, kneading until butter is incorporated and dough is smooth and elastic. Turn out dough onto floured surface; knead in pearl sugar.

4. Divide dough into 12 balls; place on plate. Cover and let rise in warm place 30 minutes.

5. Preheat waffle maker to medium. Place dough ball onto waffle maker for each waffle; cook about 2 to 3 minutes or until golden brown and crisp. Remove to plate. Repeat with remaining dough.

GRAHAM CRACKERS

MAKES ABOUT 12 CRACKERS

½ **cup sweet rice flour (mochiko)**

½ **cup sorghum flour**

½ **cup packed brown sugar**

⅓ **cup tapioca flour**

½ **teaspoon baking soda**

½ **teaspoon salt**

¼ **cup (½ stick) cold butter, cut into pieces**

2 **tablespoons plus 2 teaspoons milk**

2 **tablespoons honey**

1 **tablespoon vanilla**

1. Attach flat beater to stand mixer. Combine ½ cup sweet rice flour, sorghum flour, brown sugar, tapioca flour, baking soda and salt in mixer bowl. Add butter; mix on low speed until coarse crumbs form.

2. Whisk milk, honey and vanilla in small bowl until well blended and honey is dissolved. Add to flour mixture; mix on low speed until dough forms. (Dough will be very soft and sticky.)

3. Transfer dough to floured surface; pat into rectangle. Wrap in plastic wrap and refrigerate at least 4 hours or up to 2 days.

4. Preheat oven to 325°F. Cover work surface with parchment paper; generously dust with rice flour.

5. Roll dough to ⅛-inch-thick rectangle on parchment paper with floured rolling pin. (If dough becomes too sticky, return to refrigerator or freezer for several minutes.) Place dough on parchment paper on baking sheet. Score dough into cracker shapes; prick dough in rows with tines of fork. Place baking sheet in freezer 5 to 10 minutes or in refrigerator 15 to 20 minutes.

6. Bake chilled crackers 25 minutes or until firm and slightly darkened. Slide crackers on parchment onto wire rack to cool. Cut into crackers along score lines when cooled slightly.

PARMESAN AND PINE NUT SHORTBREAD

MAKES 26 TO 28 CRACKERS

½ **cup all-purpose flour**

⅓ **cup whole wheat flour**

⅓ **cup cornmeal**

¼ **teaspoon salt**

½ **cup (1 stick) butter, softened**

½ **cup shredded Parmesan cheese**

⅓ **cup sugar**

3 **to 5 tablespoons pine nuts**

1. Combine flours, cornmeal and salt in small bowl.

2. Attach flat beater to stand mixer. Beat butter, cheese and sugar in mixer bowl on high speed until light and fluffy. Gradually add flour mixture, beating well on low speed after each addition. Shape dough into log 8 to 10 inches long and about 2 inches in diameter. Wrap in plastic wrap; refrigerate 30 minutes.

3. Preheat oven to 375°F. Line baking sheet with parchment paper. Cut dough into ⅓-inch slices with sharp knife. Arrange 1 inch apart on prepared baking sheet. Press 3 to 5 pine nuts on each slice. Bake 11 to 13 minutes or until firm and lightly browned. Cool on baking sheet 5 minutes. Remove to wire rack; cool completely.

CRANBERRY BRIE BUBBLE BREAD

MAKES 12 SERVINGS

3 cups all-purpose flour

1 package (¼ ounce) rapid-rise active dry yeast

1 teaspoon salt

1 cup warm water (120°F)

¼ cup plus 2 tablespoons butter, melted, divided

¾ cup finely chopped pecans or walnuts

¼ cup packed brown sugar

¼ teaspoon coarse salt

1 package (7 ounces) Brie cheese, cut into ¼-inch pieces

1 cup whole-berry cranberry sauce

1. Attach dough hook to stand mixer. Combine flour, yeast and 1 teaspoon salt in mixer bowl. Stir in water and 2 tablespoons melted butter with wooden spoon to form rough dough. Knead on low speed 5 to 7 minutes or until dough is smooth and elastic.

2. Shape dough into a ball. Place in large lightly greased bowl; turn once to grease surface. Cover and let rise in warm place about 45 minutes or until doubled in size.

3. Grease 2-quart ovenproof bowl or baking dish. Combine pecans, brown sugar and coarse salt in shallow bowl. Place remaining ¼ cup melted butter in another shallow bowl. Turn out dough onto lightly floured surface; pat and stretch into 9×6-inch rectangle. Cut dough into 1-inch pieces; roll into balls.

4. Dip balls of dough in butter; roll in pecan mixture to coat. Place in prepared bowl, layering with Brie and cranberry sauce. Cover and let rise in warm place about 45 minutes or until dough is puffy.

5. Preheat oven to 350°F. Bake 30 minutes or until dough is firm and filling is bubbly. Cool on wire rack 15 to 20 minutes. Serve warm.

CHEDDAR CRISPS

MAKES ABOUT 3 DOZEN CRISPS

- 1¾ **cups all-purpose flour**
- ½ **cup yellow cornmeal**
- ¾ **teaspoon sugar**
- ¾ **teaspoon salt**
- ½ **teaspoon baking soda**
- ½ **cup (1 stick) cold butter, cut into pieces**
- 1½ **cups (6 ounces) shredded sharp Cheddar cheese**
- ½ **cup cold water**
- 2 **tablespoons white vinegar**
  Coarsely ground black pepper

1. Attach flat beater to stand mixer. Combine flour, cornmeal, sugar, salt and baking soda in mixer bowl. Add butter; mix on low speed until mixture resembles coarse crumbs. Add cheese, water and vinegar; mix on low speed until mixture forms soft dough. Wrap dough in plastic wrap; refrigerate 1 hour or freeze 30 minutes or until firm.

2. Preheat oven to 375°F. Grease two baking sheets. Divide dough into 4 pieces. Roll each piece into paper-thin circle, about 13 inches in diameter, on floured surface. Sprinkle with pepper; press firmly into dough.

3. Cut each circle into 8 wedges; place on prepared baking sheets. Bake about 10 minutes or until crisp. Store in airtight container up to 3 days.

SOFT BEER PRETZELS

MAKES 12 PRETZELS

1 package (¼ ounce) rapid-rise active dry yeast

¼ cup warm water (105°F to 115°F)

3¾ to 4 cups all-purpose flour

1 cup brown ale, at room temperature

1 tablespoon sugar

1 tablespoon olive oil

¾ teaspoon kosher salt, plus additional for topping

2 cups hot water

1 teaspoon baking soda

1 egg, well beaten

2 tablespoons butter, melted

1. Attach dough hook to stand mixer. Stir yeast into water in mixer bowl until dissolved. Let stand 5 minutes. Add 2 cups flour, beer, sugar, olive oil and ¾ teaspoon salt; knead on low speed 5 to 7 minutes or until dough is smooth and elastic, adding additional flour as needed to prevent sticking.

2. Shape dough into a ball. Place in large lightly greased bowl; turn once to grease surface. Cover and let rise in warm place 45 minutes or until doubled in size.

3. Grease baking sheet. Turn out dough onto lightly floured surface. Divide into 12 pieces. Roll each piece into rope, about 20 inches long. Shape ropes into pretzels.

4. Combine hot water and baking soda in large shallow bowl. Dip pretzels into mixture; place on prepared baking sheet. Cover loosely and let stand in warm place 15 to 20 minutes. Brush pretzels with egg; sprinkle with additional salt.

5. Preheat oven to 425°F. Bake 10 minutes or until golden brown. Brush pretzels with melted butter. Cool slightly; serve warm.

KOREAN SCALLION PANCAKE WAFFLES

MAKES 4 SERVINGS

DIPPING SAUCE

- **3 tablespoons soy sauce**
- **1½ tablespoons water**
- **2 teaspoons rice vinegar**
- **2 teaspoons dark sesame oil**
- **¾ teaspoon sugar**
- **1½ teaspoons sesame seeds**
- **½ teaspoon minced garlic**

WAFFLES

- **¾ cup all-purpose flour**
- **½ cup cornstarch**
- **½ teaspoon salt**
- **1 cup very cold water**
- **1 egg, lightly beaten**
- **½ red bell pepper, julienned into 2-inch pieces**
- **¾ cup thinly sliced green onion (2-inch pieces)**
- **2 small carrots, peeled and grated (about ¾ cup)**
- **2 teaspoons minced garlic**
- **2 teaspoons vegetable oil, plus additional for brushing**

1. Preheat classic waffle maker to medium-high heat. Preheat oven to 200°F. Set wire rack on top of large baking sheet.

2. For dipping sauce, whisk soy sauce, water, vinegar, sesame oil, sugar, sesame seeds and ½ teaspoon garlic in small bowl. Set aside.

3. For waffles, attach wire whip to stand mixer. Combine flour, cornstarch and salt in mixer bowl. Add water and egg; whip on medium speed until combined. Fold in bell pepper, green onion, carrots and 2 teaspoons garlic.

4. Brush grids of waffle maker with oil. Pour ½ cup batter into center of waffle maker; gently spread with rubber spatula to cover surface of grid. Close lid; cook 2 minutes. Open lid; drizzle ½ teaspoon oil over top of waffle; close lid and continue cooking until golden brown and crisp, about 4 to 5 minutes.

5. Remove waffles to wire rack; keep warm in oven. Repeat with remaining batter, brushing waffle maker with oil before each batch. Serve warm with dipping sauce.

A

Almond Glaze, 161
Almonds
  Almond Glaze, 161
  Banana-Coconut Cream Pie, 46
  Cherry, Almond and Chocolate Twist, 160
  Cherry-Almond Clafouti, 89
  Peach Raspberry Pie, 44
  Plum-Rhubarb Crumble, 94
Anadama Bread, 116
Apple-Pear Praline Pie, 43
Apple Ring Coffeecake, 165
Apples
  Apple Ring Coffeecake, 165
  Apple-Pear Praline Pie, 43
  English Bread Pudding, 95
  Swedish Apple Pie, 57
  Warm Apple and Blueberry Crisp, 83
Apricot
  Apricot Bars, 39
  Blueberry-Apricot Streusel Bread, 126

B

Bacon
  Caramel Nut Bacon Brownies, 35
  Caramelized Onion-Bacon Muffins, 141
  Maple Bacon Bubble Bread, 170
Bagels, 112
Banana Cake, 75
Banana-Coconut Cream Pie, 46
Banana-Pecan Swirl, 110
Bananas
  Banana Cake, 75
  Banana-Coconut Cream Pie, 46
  Banana-Pecan Swirl, 110
  Fresh Fruit Tart, 50
  Loaded Banana Bread, 124
Basic Oatmeal Cookies, 15
Beer
  Caramelized Onion-Bacon Muffins, 141
  Ginger Stout Cake, 68
  Porter Cake, 80
  Pretzel Rolls, 102

Belgian Leige Waffles, 180
Black and White Sandwich Cookies, 22
Blueberries
  Blueberry-Apricot Streusel Bread, 126
  Blueberry Crumb Cake, 69
  Blueberry Doughnuts, 139
  Blueberry Pecan Tea Bread, 136
  Blueberry Shortcake, 92
  Fresh Fruit Tart, 50
  Warm Apple and Blueberry Crisp, 83
Blueberry-Apricot Streusel Bread, 126
Blueberry Crumb Cake, 69
Blueberry Doughnuts, 139
Blueberry Pecan Tea Bread, 136
Blueberry Shortcake, 92
Boston Black Coffee Bread, 131
Brownies
  Caramel Bacon Nut Brownies, 35
  Cinnamon-Wheat Brownies, 37
  Sour Cream Brownies, 41
Buttery Frosting, 63

C

Cakes, Layer
  Banana Cake, 75
  Caramel-Topped Cream Cake, 63
  Chocolate Cake, 64
  Chocolate Espresso Cake, 70
  Chocolate Hazelnut Delight, 78
  Classic Yellow Cake, 76
Caramel
  Caramel Bacon Nut Brownies, 35
  Caramel-Topped Cream Cake, 63
  Chocolate Caramel Bars, 40
  Turtle Pecan Pie, 47
Caramel Bacon Nut Brownies, 35
Caramel-Topped Cream Cake, 63
Caramel Topping, 63
Caramelized Onion-Bacon Muffins, 141

Cardamom Rolls, 108
Cheddar Crisps, 185
Cheese
  Caramelized Onion-Bacon Muffins, 141
  Cheddar Crisps, 185
  Cranberry Brie Bubble Bread, 184
  Parmesan and Pine Nut Shortbread, 183
  Pesto Pull-Apart Swirls, 115
  Pull-Apart Garlic Cheese Bread, 175
  Spanikopita Pull-Aparts, 101
Cheesecake: Marbled Pumpkin Cheesecake, 66
Cherries
  Cherry, Almond and Chocolate Twist, 160
  Cherry-Almond Clafouti, 89
  Cherry Buttermilk Loops, 166
  Cherry-Lemon Poppy Seed Muffins, 155
  Cherry Pink Cupcakes, 72
  Cherry Pink Frosting, 72
  Lattice-Topped Cherry Pie, 53
Cherry, Almond and Chocolate Twist, 160
Cherry-Almond Clafouti, 89
Cherry Buttermilk Loops, 166
Cherry-Lemon Poppy Seed Muffins, 155
Cherry Pink Cupcakes, 72
Cherry Pink Frosting, 72
Chocolate
  Banana Cake, 75
  Black and White Sandwich Cookies, 22
  Caramel Bacon Nut Brownies, 35
  Cherry, Almond and Chocolate Twist, 160
  Chocolate Buttercream Frosting, 70
  Chocolate Cake, 64
  Chocolate Caramel Bars, 40
  Chocolate Chip Skillet Cookie, 30
  Chocolate-Coconut-Toffee Cookies, 18
  Chocolate Crème Brûlée, 88
  Chocolate Curls, 58

Chocolate (continued)
Chocolate Dream Bars, 38
Chocolate Espresso Cake, 70
Chocolate Hazelnut Delight, 78
Chocolate Peanut Butter Doughnuts, 90
Chocolate-Raspberry Bread Pudding, 84
Chocolate Raspberry Thumbprints, 27
Cinnamon-Wheat Brownies, 37
Classic Chocolate Chip Cookies, 9
Cocoa Crackles, 26
Deep Dark Chocolate Drops, 20
Easy Layered Bars, 33
Espresso Chocolate Frosting, 70
Ganache Frosting, 64
Loaded Banana Bread, 124
Marbled Pumpkin Cheesecake, 66
Mini Pain au Chocolate, 177
Mississippi Mud Bars, 32
Mocha Brownie Cookies, 17
Mocha Cinnamon Blondies, 31
Sour Cream Brownies, 41
Sour Cream Doughnuts, 148
Toffee Bars, 34
Triple Chocolate Sticky Buns, 162
Turtle Pecan Pie, 47
Chocolate Buttercream Frosting, 70
Chocolate Cake, 64
Chocolate Caramel Bars, 40
Chocolate Chip Skillet Cookie, 30
Chocolate-Coconut-Toffee Cookies, 18
Chocolate Crème Brûlée, 88
Chocolate Curls, 58
Chocolate Dream Bars, 38
Chocolate Espresso Cake, 70
Chocolate Hazelnut Delight, 78
Chocolate Peanut Butter Doughnuts, 90
Chocolate-Raspberry Bread Pudding, 84
Chocolate Raspberry Thumbprints, 27

Cinnamini Monkey Bread, 159
Cinnamon Raisin Bread, 118
Cinnamon Rolls, 106
Cinnamon-Wheat Brownies, 37
Citrus Bread, 133
Classic Chocolate Chip Cookies, 9
Classic Thumbprints, 16
Classic Yellow Cake, 76
Cocoa Crackles, 26
Coconut
Banana-Coconut Cream Pie, 46
Chocolate-Coconut-Toffee Cookies, 18
Coconut Scones with Orange Butter, 156
Easy Layered Bars, 33
Loaded Banana Bread, 124
Coconut Scones with Orange Butter, 156
Coffee
Boston Black Coffee Bread, 131
Chocolate Espresso Cake, 70
Espresso Chocolate Frosting, 70
Mocha Brownie Cookies, 17
Mocha Cinnamon Blondies, 31
Cookies, Drop
Basic Oatmeal Cookies, 15
Classic Chocolate Chip Cookies, 9
Deep Dark Chocolate Drops, 20
Mocha Brownie Cookies, 17
Pumpkin White Chocolate Drops, 12
Cookies, Cutout and Shaped
Black and White Sandwich Cookies, 22
Chocolate-Coconut-Toffee Cookies, 18
Chocolate Raspberry Thumbprints, 27
Classic Thumbprints, 16
Cocoa Crackles, 26
Gingerbread Letters, 24
Ginger Molasses Thins, 10
Refrigerator Cookies, 21
Shortbread Cookies, 11
Snickerdoodles, 14
Corn Bread, 130

Corn Muffins, 130
Country Pecan Pie, 56
Cranberries
Cranberry Brie Bubble Bread, 184
Cranberry Pound Cake, 81
Cranberry Pumpkin Nut Bread, 123
Cranberry Brie Bubble Bread, 184
Cranberry Pound Cake, 81
Cranberry Pumpkin Nut Bread, 123
Creamy White Frosting, 76
Crunch Peach Cobbler, 96
Crunchy Whole Grain Bread, 120
Cupcakes: Cherry Pink Cupcakes, 72

D
Date Nut Bread, 128
Dates
Date Nut Bread, 128
Zucchini Bread, 129
Doughnuts
Blueberry Doughnuts, 152
Chocolate Peanut Butter Doughnuts, 90
Lemon-Filled Doughnuts, 152
Sour Cream Doughnuts, 148
Sugar and Spice Doughnuts, 144
Deep Dark Chocolate Drops, 20

E
Easy Layered Bars, 33
Egg Bagels, 104
English Bread Pudding, 95
English-Style Scones, 146
Espresso Chocolate Frosting, 70

F
Fresh Fruit Tart, 50
Frostings and Glazes
Almond Glaze, 161
Buttery Frosting, 63
Caramel Topping, 63
Cherry Pink Frosting, 72
Chocolate Buttercream Frosting, 70
Creamy White Frosting, 76

Frostings and Glazes
(continued)
Espresso Chocolate Frosting, 70
Ganache Frosting, 64
Honey Butter, 130
Lemon Curd, 126
Meringue Powder Icing, 24
Orange Butter, 156
Sweetened Whipped Cream, 58

G
Ganache Frosting, 64
Ginger
Gingerbread Letters, 24
Ginger Molasses Thins, 10
Gingersnap Cookie Crust, 66
Ginger Stout Cake, 68
Marbled Pumpkin Cheesecake, 66
Gingerbread Letters, 24
Ginger Molasses Thins, 10
Gingersnap Cookie Crust, 66
Ginger Stout Cake, 68
Graham Crackers, 182

H
Hazelnuts: Chocolate Hazelnut Delight, 78
Honey Butter, 130
Honey Butter Pull-Apart Bread, 176

I
Irish Soda Bread, 132
Italian Chocolate Pie alla Lucia, 58

K
Korean Scallion Pancake Waffles, 187

L
Lattice-Topped Cherry Pie, 53
Lemon
Cherry-Lemon Poppy Seed Muffins, 155
Citrus Bread, 133
Lemon Curd, 126

Lemon *(continued)*
Lemon-Filled Doughnuts, 152
Lemon Meringue Pie, 54
Lemon Poppy Seed Muffins, 142
Lemon Squares, 29
Lemon Tart, 48
Tangy Lemon Raspberry Bars, 36
Lemon Curd, 126
Lemon-Filled Doughnuts, 152
Lemon Meringue Pie, 54
Lemon Poppy Seed Muffins, 142
Lemon Squares, 29
Lemon Tart, 48
Loaded Banana Bread, 124

M
Maple
Maple Bacon Bubble Bread, 170
Maple Pecan Tart, 52
Maple Bacon Bubble Bread, 170
Maple Pecan Tart, 52
Marbled Pumpkin Cheesecake, 66
Meringue Powder Icing, 24
Mini Pain au Chocolate, 177
Mini Strawberry Shortcakes, 86
Mississippi Mud Bars, 32
Mocha Brownie Cookies, 17
Mocha Cinnamon Blondies, 31
Muffins
Cherry-Lemon Poppy Seed Muffins, 155
Lemon Poppy Seed Muffins, 140
Peanut Butter Bran Muffins, 154
Pumpkin Pecan Muffins, 142
Raspberry Corn Muffins, 147
Streusel Raspberry Muffins

N
No-Knead Sandwich Bread, 114

O
Oats
Apricot Bars, 39
Basic Oatmeal Cookies, 15
Crunch Peach Cobbler, 96

Oats *(continued)*
Crunchy Whole Grain Bread, 120
Easy Layered Bars, 33
Peach Raspberry Pie, 44
Plum-Rhubarb Crumble, 94
Strawberry-Rhubarb Crisp, 85
Tangy Lemon Raspberry Bars, 36
Warm Apple and Blueberry Crisp, 83
Orange
Citrus Bread, 133
Coconut Scones with Orange Butter, 156
Italian Chocolate Pie alla Lucia, 58
Orange-Almond Pound Cake, 74
Orange Butter, 156
Orange-Currant Scones, 151
Orange Poppy Seed Sweet Rolls, 164
Porter Cake, 80
Orange-Almond Pound Cake, 74
Orange Butter, 156
Orange-Currant Scones, 151
Orange Poppy Seed Sweet Rolls, 164

P
Parmesan and Pine Nut Shortbread, 183
Pastry for Double-Crust Pie, 43
Pastry for Single-Crust Pie, 44
Peach Raspberry Pie, 44
Peaches
Crunch Peach Cobbler, 96
Fresh Fruit Tart, 50
Peach Raspberry Pie, 44
Peanut Butter Bran Muffins, 154
Peanuts and Peanut Butter
Chocolate Peanut Butter Doughnuts, 90
Peanut Butter Bran Muffins, 154
Pears: Apple-Pear Praline Pie, 43
Pecan-Cinnamon Sticky Buns, 168
Pecans
Apple-Pear Praline Pie, 43
Banana-Pecan Swirl, 110

Pecans (continued)

Blueberry Pecan Tea Bread, 136

Caramel Bacon Nut Brownies, 35

Cherry-Lemon Poppy Seed Muffins, 155

Chocolate Caramel Bars, 40

Country Pecan Pie, 56

Easy Layered Bars, 33

Maple Pecan Tart, 52

Mocha Cinnamon Blondies, 31

Pecan-Cinnamon Sticky Buns, 168

Praline Pumpkin Tart, 60

Pumpkin Pecan Muffins, 140

Streusel Raspberry Muffins, 150

Turtle Pecan Pie, 47

Pesto Pull-Apart Swirls, 115

Pineapple: Loaded Banana Bread, 124

Plum-Rhubarb Crumble, 94

Porter Cake, 80

Praline Pumpkin Tart, 60

Pretzel Bites with Honey Mustard, 178

Pretzel Rolls, 102

Pretzels

Pretzel Bites with Honey Mustard, 178

Pretzel Rolls, 102

Soft Beer Pretzels, 186

Pull-Apart Breads

Cinnamini Monkey Bread, 159

Cranberry Brie Bubble Bread, 184

Honey Butter Pull-Apart Bread, 176

Maple Bacon Bubble Bread, 170

Pesto Pull-Apart Swirls, 115

Pull-Apart Garlic Cheese Bread, 175

Spanikopita Pull-Aparts, 101

Pull-Apart Garlic Cheese Bread, 175

Pumpkin

Cranberry Pumpkin Nut Bread, 123

Marbled Pumpkin Cheesecake, 66

Praline Pumpkin Tart, 60

Pumpkin (continued)

Pumpkin Pecan Muffins, 140

Pumpkin White Chocolate Drops, 12

Pumpkin Pecan Muffins, 140

Pumpkin White Chocolate Drops, 12

R

Raisins

Cinnamon Raisin Bread, 118

Easy Layered Bars, 33

English-Style Scones, 146

Irish Soda Bread, 132

Peanut Butter Bran Muffins, 154

Porter Cake, 80

Wheat Germ Bread, 137

Raspberries

Chocolate-Raspberry Bread Pudding, 84

Chocolate Raspberry Thumbprints, 27

Fresh Fruit Tart, 50

Peach Raspberry Pie, 44

Raspberry Breakfast Ring, 172

Raspberry Corn Muffins, 147

Streusel Raspberry Muffins, 150

Tangy Lemon Raspberry Bars, 36

Raspberry Breakfast Ring, 172

Raspberry Corn Muffins, 147

Refrigerator Cookies, 21

Rhubarb

Plum-Rhubarb Crumble, 94

Rhubarb Bread, 134

Strawberry-Rhubarb Crisp, 85

Strawberry-Rhubarb Pie, 49

Rhubarb Bread, 134

S

Scones

Coconut Scones with Orange Butter, 156

English-Style Scones, 146

Orange-Currant Scones, 151

Shortbread Cookies, 11

Snickerdoodles, 14

Soft Beer Pretzels, 186

Sour Cream Brownies, 41

Sour Cream Doughnuts, 148

Spanikopita Pull-Aparts, 101

Strawberries

Classic Thumbprints, 16

Fresh Fruit Tart, 50

Mini Strawberry Shortcakes, 86

Strawberry-Rhubarb Crisp, 85

Strawberry-Rhubarb Pie, 49

Strawberry-Rhubarb Crisp, 85

Strawberry-Rhubarb Pie, 49

Streusel Raspberry Muffins, 150

Sugar and Spice Doughnuts, 144

Swedish Apple Pie, 57

Sweetened Whipped Cream, 58

T

Tangy Lemon Raspberry Bars, 36

Toffee Bars, 34

Triple Chocolate Sticky Buns, 162

Turtle Pecan Pie, 47

W

Waffles

Belgian Leige Waffles, 180

Korean Scallion Pancake Waffles, 187

Walnuts

Apple Ring Coffeecake, 165

Blueberry Crumb Cake, 69

Chocolate Dream Bars, 38

Cinnamon-Wheat Brownies, 37

Date Nut Bread, 128

Mississippi Mud Bars, 32

Rhubarb Bread, 134

Toffee Bars, 34

Triple Chocolate Sticky Buns, 162

Warm Apple and Blueberry Crisp, 83

Wheat Germ Bread, 137

White Chocolate

Mississippi Mud Bars, 32

Pumpkin White Chocolate Drops, 12

Z

Zucchini Bread, 129

METRIC CONVERSION CHART

VOLUME MEASUREMENTS (dry)

⅛ teaspoon = 0.5 mL
¼ teaspoon = 1 mL
½ teaspoon = 2 mL
¾ teaspoon = 4 mL
1 teaspoon = 5 mL
1 tablespoon = 15 mL
2 tablespoons = 30 mL
¼ cup = 60 mL
⅓ cup = 75 mL
½ cup = 125 mL
⅔ cup = 150 mL
¾ cup = 175 mL
1 cup = 250 mL
2 cups = 1 pint = 500 mL
3 cups = 750 mL
4 cups = 1 quart = 1 L

VOLUME MEASUREMENTS (fluid)

1 fluid ounce (2 tablespoons) = 30 mL
4 fluid ounces (½ cup) = 125 mL
8 fluid ounces (1 cup) = 250 mL
12 fluid ounces (1½ cups) = 375 mL
16 fluid ounces (2 cups) = 500 mL

WEIGHTS (mass)

½ ounce = 15 g
1 ounce = 30 g
3 ounces = 90 g
4 ounces = 120 g
8 ounces = 225 g
10 ounces = 285 g
12 ounces = 360 g
16 ounces = 1 pound = 450 g

DIMENSIONS

1/16 inch = 2 mm
⅛ inch = 3 mm
¼ inch = 6 mm
½ inch = 1.5 cm
¾ inch = 2 cm
1 inch = 2.5 cm

OVEN TEMPERATURES

250°F = 120°C
275°F = 140°C
300°F = 150°C
325°F = 160°C
350°F = 180°C
375°F = 190°C
400°F = 200°C
425°F = 220°C
450°F = 230°C

BAKING PAN SIZES

Utensil	Size in Inches/Quarts	Metric Volume	Size in Centimeters
Baking or Cake Pan (square or rectangular)	8×8×2	2 L	20×20×5
	9×9×2	2.5 L	23×23×5
	12×8×2	3 L	30×20×5
	13×9×2	3.5 L	33×23×5
Loaf Pan	8×4×3	1.5 L	20×10×7
	9×5×3	2 L	23×13×7
Round Layer Cake Pan	8×1½	1.2 L	20×4
	9×1½	1.5 L	23×4
Pie Plate	8×1¼	750 mL	20×3
	9×1¼	1 L	23×3
Baking Dish or Casserole	1 quart	1 L	—
	1½ quart	1.5 L	—
	2 quart	2 L	—